CHURCH HIST

SETBACK AND RECOVERY
AD 500–1500

TEF Study Guides

This SPCK series was first sponsored by the Theological Education Fund of the WCC in response to requests from colleges in Africa, the Caribbean and South Pacific. The Guides continue to be written by and in consultation with theological tutors from all over the world, but have from the outset been as widely used by students and parish groups in the West as by those for whom English may be a second language. More advanced titles in the list are marked (A).

General Editors: Daphne Terry and Nicholas Beddow

TEF Study Guide 8

CHURCH HISTORY 2
SETBACK AND RECOVERY
AD 500–1500

JOHN FOSTER

First published in 1974
SPCK
Holy Trinity Church
Marylebone Road, London NW1 4DU

Ninth Impression 1991

ISBN 0 281 02789 7 (net edition)
ISBN 0 281 02790 0 (non-edition for Africa,
Asia, S. Pacific and Caribbean)

Printed by offset in Great Britain by
Hollen Street Press Ltd. Slough, Berks.

Contents

CONTENTS

CONTENTS

Illustrations, maps, and charts

ILLUSTRATIONS, MAPS, AND CHARTS

ACKNOWLEDGEMENTS

The photographs and other pictures in this book are reproduced by permission of Camera Press Ltd (7.5 and 7.6) and the Mansell Collection, London. The graph in Chart 4 is based, by permission, on a similar graph in K. S. Latourette's *History of Christianity*.

x

Editor's Note:
The plan and use of this book

WHAT KIND OF CHURCH HISTORY?

As noted in Part 1, teachers of Church History in colleges where the TEF series is likely to be used were consulted before it was decided what approach to the subject should be adopted in these Guides. The replies received made it clear that no single book could serve all their various needs. But in most of the colleges concerned, teaching is still on traditional 'chronological' lines, with Latourette's *History of Christianity* or books on a similar pattern as the standard textbooks most widely used at degree and diploma level. That approach, therefore, is the one which John Foster decided on for this four-part history.

This present volume, *Setback and Recovery*, is Part 2. It covers the 'thousand years of uncertainty'—AD 500–1500—and is concerned among other emphases with the developing reality of 'Christendom', the rise and fall of the Papacy as a focus of political power, and the long struggle between Christendom and Islam. Part 1, *The First Advance*, covered the first 500 years of the Church's spread, not only westward, but farther into Asia and into Africa. Part 3, *New Movements*, examines the period 1500-1800, when new movements of reform and revolution were setting the stage for the great missionary expansion of the 19th century and the growth of autonomous national Churches around the world in our own time, which are the subject of Part 4: *Christianity Worldwide*.

SOURCE MATERIALS

A companion reference volume of extracts from original source documents was considered. But W. G. Young's *Handbook of Source Materials for Students of Church History*, published by the CLS, Madras, fulfils the need fairly well for the first of the TEF volumes. For this reason, and to help students working on their own or without easy access to reference books, it was decided not to issue a separate TEF Source Book, but to include as an integral part of the Study Guides, extracts from the more important sources quoted.

However, all students who can are strongly advised to obtain for themselves a copy of Young's *Handbook*. In Part I of this History, as in this present volume, the quotation reference numbers in bold type correspond to the numbered extracts in Young, and students may find it helpful to read the more extensive extracts there as they go along.

A list of the standard reference books in which other source material is likely to be found is noted in the Bibliography, p. xiv, and students with access to a library may wish to follow up these sources also.

Many of the extracts quoted have been specially translated or abbreviated by the author for inclusion in this History.

MAPS, CHARTS, AND PICTURES

Most of the place-names mentioned in the book can be found on one or other of the *maps* which appear at appropriate points in the text.

The unified *time charts*, pp. 54 and 126, show comparative dates of people and events important in the history of the Church during the period covered.

The *pictures* show something of the more important people and events of that period, and are drawn, as far as possible, from the work of artists who themselves lived at that time.

STUDY SUGGESTIONS

Suggestions for further study appear at the end of each chapter. They are intended to help readers to study more thoroughly and to understand more clearly what they have read. They also provide topics for group research and discussion. They are of three main sorts:

1. *Word studies.* These will help readers to check and deepen their understanding of any technical or other special terms which it has been necessary to use.

2. *Review questions* on the content of the chapter. These will help readers to check their progress and ensure that they have fully grasped and remembered the ideas discussed and the facts presented. The answers should be written down, and then checked with the Key (p. 189).

3. *Questions for further study, research, and discussion.* These will help readers to understand why things happened as they did; to discover for themselves the links between the life of the medieval Church and the lives of Christians today; and to consider the ways in which their own actions may affect the development of the Church in the future.

Please note that the Study Suggestions are only *suggestions*. Some readers may not want to use them at all. Some teachers may want to use them selectively, or to substitute alternative questions of their own.

The *Key* (p. 189) will enable readers to check their own work on those questions which can be checked in this way. In most cases the Key does not give the answer to a question; it shows where an answer is to be found.

EDITOR'S NOTE

INDEX

The Index (p. 199) includes all the proper names of important people and places mentioned, and the main subjects dealt with.

BIBLE VERSION

The English translation of the Bible used and quoted in this book is the Revised Standard Version (RSV).

THE AUTHOR

To our great sorrow Dr John Foster, who had undertaken to prepare all the volumes of this history, was taken ill, and died shortly after this second volume had been sent to the printer. He had suffered some ill-health while working on it, and we can only be thankful that he lived long enough to see the MS complete. If in any respect the book falls short of the high standard he set for Volume 1, it will be for lack of his eagle eye upon it during the final stages of preparation.

To find at short notice an alternative author for Volume 3 seemed a daunting prospect, till we learned that unexpected visa problems would give Dr Alan Thomson some time to spare in the coming year. We are very grateful indeed for his willingness to take up the task where Dr Foster left off. He also contributes a section to Volume 4, which is planned as a symposium by authors from the main regions of the world covered.

Bibliography

Readers may find the following books useful for further study:

GENERAL

Addison, J. T., *The Medieval Missionary*. Philadelphia, Porcupine Press, 1977.

Chadwick, H., *The Early Church*. Harmondsworth, Penguin, 1968.

Deanesly, M., *A History of the Medieval Church*. London, Methuen, 1969.

Gibbs, M. E., *From Jerusalem to New Delhi*. Madras, Christian Literature Society.

Hamilton, B., *Religion in the Medieval West*. London, E. Arnold, 1986.

Latourette, K. S., *A History of Christianity*. New York and London, Harper and Row, 1976.

Lawrence, C. H., *Medieval Monasticism*. Harlow, Longman, 1984.

Lights and Shades of Christendom, vols. 1 and 2. Delhi, ISPCK.

Southern, R. W., *Western Society and the Church in the Middle Ages*. Harmondsworth, Penguin, 1970.

SOURCE AND REFERENCE BOOKS

Bede, *A History of the English Church and People*. London, Penguin.

Bettenson, H. S., *Documents of the Christian Church*. New York, OUP, 1967.

Cross, F. L., *Oxford Dictionary of the Christian Church*. Oxford, OUP, 1974.

Stevenson, J., *A New Eusebius*. Documents illustrating the history of the Church to AD 337, Rev. by W. H. C. Frend with additional material. SPCK, 1987.

Stevenson, J., *Creeds, Councils and Controversies*. Documents illustrating the history of the Church AD 337–461. Rev. by W. H. C. Frend. SPCK, 1989.

Young, W. G., *Handbook of Source Materials for Students of Church History (to AD 650)*. Madras, Christian Literature Society, 1969.

CHAPTER 1

Setback in the West:
Fall of the Western Roman Empire

One striking sign of the Christian religion's progress in its first five hundred years is the church which is often called 'the church of Saint Sophia' in Constantinople. It is more correct to translate its name as 'the church of the holy Wisdom'. *Sophia* is the Greek word for 'wisdom', and the church was dedicated to Christ as the Wisdom of God. It was built by the Roman Emperor Justinian I between 532 and 537.

Procopius, an official in Constantinople at that time, described it:

'A building incomparably beautiful, it seems not just to stand upon its foundations, but to cover wide space, with its golden dome hung down from heaven.' (Procopius, *On Buildings*)

Most earlier churches had been rectangular buildings with rows of pillars down the middle to support the roof. The builders of this new church widened the span of the roof by standing the dome on half-domes, so that there are fewer pillars which obstruct the view. After fourteen centuries it remains one of the most wonderful churches ever built (see p. 3). Its magnificence seems far removed from the simple house-churches of the first Christians.

Yet if the two architects, both men from Asia Minor, had been asked why they were so careful not to obstruct the view, they would have said that it was meant to recall the Upper Room of a Jerusalem house where Jesus took bread and wine and said to his followers, 'Do this in remembrance of me' (1 Cor. 11.25). Here in Constantinople the Eucharist was no longer celebrated within sight of the congregation. People had come to feel that it was more reverent to hide the altar behind a curtain. But the Eucharist was the crown of Christian worship, and taking the bread and wine was still the sign of Christ's presence. So on the curtain, richly embroidered, was a picture of Christ, and the vast congregation all looked towards that. In this most wonderful building the simplest definition of our religion was still true, 'Christianity is Christ' (see Vol. 1, p. 134).

CHRISTIANITY'S TRIUMPH

The first congregation in Jerusalem had continued to meet in the Upper Room: the Apostles, 'with the women, and Mary the mother of Jesus, and with his brothers . . . in all about a hundred and twenty' (Acts 1.13–15). Christians were then a tiny sect within the national religion of the Jews. Paul and other missionaries broke those narrow limits by preaching that Jesus was not only the long-expected Messiah of the Jews, but the Saviour of all men. More and more non-Jews became Christians, 'beginning from Jerusalem' (Vol. 1, p. 3) but spreading in all directions. There were groups of Christians here and there along the Asian, African, and European coasts of the Mediterranean Sea. Soon in Asia Minor, Syria, and Egypt, there were Christians in considerable numbers; and strong Churches in the greatest cities, Antioch, Alexandria, Rome.

About the year 180, for the first time a king became Christian, with most of the people of his small kingdom of Edessa, in Mesopotamia. By the conversion of their kings, Armenia became a Christian country about 290, and Ethiopia before 350. Ethiopia is still Christian-ruled today.

In 312 the Roman Emperor Constantine entered Rome under a Christian standard; and from that time on, the Christian cause advanced in lands all round the Mediterranean Sea.

To the east of the Roman Empire the Christians in Persia, after severe persecutions, gradually became a recognized minority. And there were scattered Christian outposts further to the east, in Bactria, India, and Ceylon.

Justinian, the same Roman Emperor who had built the wonderful church in Constantinople, commanded that the pagan temples, which had been closed, should never open again. And in 529 he closed the schools of Greek philosophy in Athens, which had been the source of pre-Christian learning.

In all the Roman Empire Christianity's triumph seemed to be complete. Yet the title of this volume has as its first word, not 'triumph', but 'setback', and the period of setback began around the year 500. If a man is made captain of a ship, he seems to have a secure future. But if, as captain, he finds that the ship is sinking, he may have no future at all. The Christian religion came to complete triumph in the Roman Empire at a time when the Empire itself, especially its western half, was breaking up. Justinian tried throughout his reign to save the Empire, and sometimes he seemed successful. But his trying used up the Empire's remaining strength, and hastened its fall. New German kingdoms were taking the place of Roman provinces (map 1, p. 6). In the west the future belonged to the Germans.

BARBARIAN INVASIONS

These German tribes had been living to the north of the river Danube and to the east of the river Rhine, the two rivers which were the frontiers

'One striking sign of the Christian religion's early progress is the church of St Sophia, built by the Roman Emperor Justinian in Constantinople between 532 and 537.' (p. 1)

1.1 When Constantinople fell to the Turks in 1453 St Sophia became a mosque, as shown in this nineteenth-century lithograph. (See also p. 184)

1.2 The mosaic portrait of Justinian in the church of St Vitale in Ravenna dates from the same century as St Sophia

3

of the Roman Empire. The Romans called the Germans *barbari* (Latin) or *barbaroi* (Greek). These were sound-words, meaning 'people whose language sounds like *bar-bar*', instead of the smooth-flowing Latin or Greek. This is the origin of the English word 'barbarian'.

The Germans had been pressing upon the frontiers of the Empire for a long time, and when they became too many to be kept out, more and more of them crossed the frontier and settled within the Empire. So, in the fifth century, *bar-bar* were the sounds heard in many parts of Italy, from farmers in the fields, from soldiers in the army, even from their officers.

From 493 onwards the ruler of Italy was Theodoric. He had this Greek name, and ruled as representing the Roman Empire in Constantinople. But he was king of the Eastern Goths. He admired the Roman Empire and all its ways, and he wanted to preserve it, not to destroy it. That was why he repaired the great Roman aqueducts and public buildings, and gave Italy thirty-six years of peaceful rule. But the fact remains that Italy, the country where Roman civilization began, had become a Gothic kingdom.

Besides the Eastern Goths, many other German tribes were moving into Roman territory. Among early invaders were the Vandals. They fought and pillaged their way through Gaul and Spain, founded a kingdom on the North African coast, and became the dreaded pirates of the Mediterranean Sea. They hated everything Roman. So they kept themselves apart from the people whom they had conquered, and learned nothing from their higher civilization. The Vandals were mere destroyers, until in 533 the Emperor Justinian sent a fleet and ten thousand soldiers to North Africa and destroyed the Vandal kingdom. He destroyed it so completely that the Vandals disappeared from history, leaving no trace, except the word 'vandalism', which is still used in most European languages to mean 'wilful or ignorant destruction of works of art'.

The Western Goths invaded southern Gaul, and soon had spread over most of Spain as well. They did not pretend to preserve the Roman Empire, as the Eastern Goths did, because they believed that it was dead and done for. Nor were they mere destroyers like the Vandals. They seized two-thirds of the land, i.e. land previously held by Gallic or Spanish farmers under Roman rule. They did allow the former inhabitants who were in positions of responsibility to continue local government and society, as in Roman times. But these inhabitants were now poorer, and civilization was in decline.

The Burgundians who settled in south-east Gaul between Eastern Goths and Western Goths behaved much as the Western Goths did. The Burgundians gave their name to Burgundy, which was later absorbed into the lands of the Franks.

4

The Franks, who had been living for a long time on the banks of the Rhine, crossed the river and began to settle in north Gaul. In 481 Clovis, a boy of fifteen, succeeded his father as their tribal chief. In 486 he defeated a Roman army, and took 'Roman' stragglers, most of whom were Germans of some kind, into his own army. Much of the land was deserted because of the troubled times, so Clovis settled his Franks upon it without displacing the local populations.

From his capital Paris, Clovis ruled over a great and growing kingdom. He guarded his eastern frontier against other German tribes. In 493 he married the daughter of the King of the Burgundians, a useful ally to the south. And he extended his rule westwards to the Atlantic Ocean and southward to the Pyrenees. Roman Gaul had become the Kingdom of the Franks, i.e. France, the strongest and most vigorous of the new nations.

THE EMPIRE IN RUINS

So, as the year 500 approached, in Italy and all lands to the west and south the Roman Empire was crumbling, falling, and being replaced by 'barbarian' kingdoms. And this was the Empire which for nearly two hundred years—ever since the pro-Christian Emperor Constantine entered Rome in the year 312—had been the scene of Christianity's chief triumphs. The question arises, was the Christian religion also doomed to crumble, fall, and be replaced by paganism?

One tragic sign of the Empire's decline had come as early as the year 410, when Alaric the Western Goth captured Rome and gave it to his army to loot. Romans said then that for eight hundred years no enemy had entered their gates, but after one hundred years of Christian rule the city had fallen. The old pagan gods seemed to have protected the city better than the God of the Christians had done. Augustine, in his book *The City of God*, had answered that, if the Christian religion had not saved Rome, it had brought to the horrors of war a new factor. Among the barbarians there were Christians who led women and children to the churches, where they were safe from attack (Vol. 1, p. 127).

We are now considering the situation another hundred years later, when Barbarians were overrunning the whole of the Western Empire. Could the presence of Christians among the barbarians again be the saving factor? Might the Christian religion survive the invasion because many of the invaders were Christians?

There were two reasons for doubting whether this would happen:

1. First, the German people who were influenced by Christianity either before or soon after they entered Roman territory, had in almost every case chosen *Arian* Christianity. The chief reason for this was that it was an Arian missionary who had been the first (about 341) to

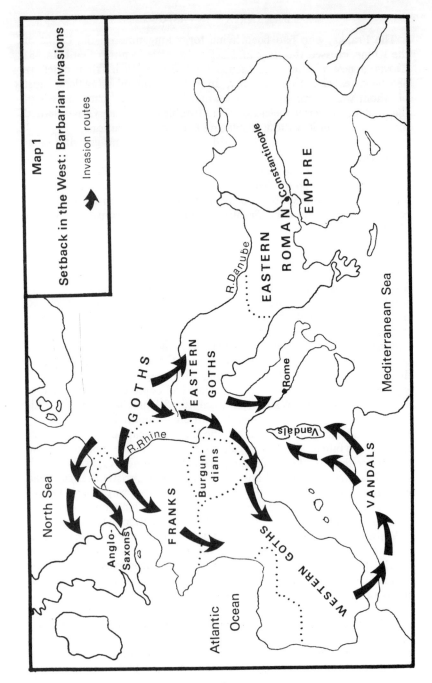

Map 1

Setback in the West: Barbarian Invasions

➤ Invasion routes

Atlantic Ocean

North Sea

Anglo-Saxons

FRANKS

R.Rhine

Burgun-dians

G O T H S

EASTERN GOTHS

WESTERN GOTHS

VANDALS

Vandals

Rome

R.Danube

EASTERN ROMAN EMPIRE

Constantinople

Mediterranean Sea

translate the Bible and Liturgy into a German language (Vol. 1, p. 122). Arius had taught that Jesus was neither fully divine nor really human. He had thought of Him as pagan peoples thought of a 'demi-god'. Thus the peoples whose land was invaded could not feel that their religion was one with that of the invaders—full Christians and Arians must go their separate ways. So the Christian position was gradually weakened by division, and where Arians became the majority, the standard of the Faith was lowered. There must be serious loss. Could Christianity recover from such a set-back?

2. And second, while we have mentioned Christians among the barbarians, there were two exceptions, the Franks and the Anglo-Saxons. Among these there had been no Christian influences—they were pagan. In the northern lands which these peoples invaded, would Christianity survive at all?

A CATHOLIC KING

The two questions were answered, both together, in 496. Clovis, king of the Franks, was baptized, and baptized by a bishop of the Catholic (i.e. whole) Church, not the Arian sect. A Church historian of the nineteenth century wrote of this conversion:

> 'It may seem a trivial occasion . . . He was the chief of only about 4,000 warriors . . . He had been influenced by his Christian wife, and by victory after praying to her God . . . But it was the most important event in European history.' (Summary of Milman, *History of Latin Christianity*, Vol. 1, p. 348)

That may be an overstatement, but the conversion of the Franks was at least, after the setback, the turning point. So we had better see how it happened.

Gregory, bishop of Tours, wrote *The History of the Franks* about the year 570 'for those who are in despair because the end of the world draws near'. The times did seem as bad as that. Gregory says that Clovis's wife, Clotilda, was a Burgundian Catholic (i.e. not an Arian), who 'never ceased warning him that he should acknowledge the true God and forsake idols'. Many later historians have rejected Gregory's account because here he names Mars, Jupiter, and Mercury, i.e. not German gods at all, but gods of pre-Christian Rome. The German gods have left their mark in the days of the week as named in many European languages. After *Sun*day and Mon(i.e. Moon)day, come Tiu, Woden, Thor (Tuesday, Wednesday, Thursday), and these are the god of war, the chief of all the gods, and the god of thunder. Roman custom had always been to seek to identify the gods of other nations with their own. Gregory, a Christian bishop, was writing in Latin, so

7

he wrote the Roman names for the war god (Mars), the chief god (Jupiter), and the thunder god (Mercury), but he meant Tiu, Woden, and Thor. So we need not question his account. Nor need we doubt him when he says that Clotilda persuaded Clovis to allow her two babies to be baptized—a child's baptism has often been the first step towards the baptism of the father.

Gregory describes Clovis turning to his wife's God when threatened with defeat in this way:

'I humbly flee to Thee for aid.
I will believe in Thee.
For I have called upon my own gods,
but they are far from my help.'   (Kidd, *Documents* III, p. 10)

This was childish bargaining with God, but it is a common way among beginners. Gregory goes on to describe the scene as the bishop of Reims, who had himself prepared Clovis for baptism, led him into the great church:

'The aisles were hung with embroidered curtains,
The baptistry was prepared with perfumes sprinkled,
Candles blazed and shone.
The whole sanctuary was fragrant, like Paradise itself.
The King went to the font, a new Constantine . . .
As he stepped into the water, the bishop spoke to the man of violence
  "Gently bow your head.
  Burn what you have worshipped.
  Worship what before you burned." '   (Kidd, *Documents* III, p. 10)

Was Clovis really converted? It is difficult to find any evidence that he became gentler or more virtuous. But here was the chance for the Church in this new kingdom of France which already stretched from the Mediterranean to the English channel, from the Atlantic ocean to the river Rhine, and which would advance eastwards. The Church would play a great part in the life of France all through the Middle Ages.

STUDY SUGGESTIONS

WORD STUDY

1. What does the Greek word *sophia* mean?
2. (a) What is the origin of the word 'barbarian'?
   (b) What is the origin of the word 'vandalism', and what does it mean?

3. Who or what were Tiu, Woden, and Thor, and in what way are we reminded of them today?
4. What does the word 'Catholic' mean as used in this chapter, and how does this differ from any way or ways in which the word is used today?

REVIEW OF CONTENT

5. (a) Which Roman emperor built the church of Saint Sophia in Constantinople?
   (b) In what way was the architecture of the church of Saint Sophia different from that of most earlier churches?
   (c) In what chief way was the celebration of the Eucharist in Saint Sophia different from the celebration of the Eucharist in early Christian house-churches?
6. 'The Roman emperor Justinian commanded that the pagan temples should never open again.' (p. 2)
   What else did Justinian close down in order to help forward the triumph of the Christian religion?
7. In about what year did the first period of setback for Christianity begin?
8. 'Italy had become a Gothic kingdom.' (p. 4)
   What is meant by this statement, and how did it happen?
9. 'Theodoric, king of the Eastern Goths, admired the Roman Empire and wanted to preserve it.' (p. 4)
   In what ways did Theodoric's attitude and actions differ from those of (a) the Western Goths, and (b) the Vandals, when they invaded the Roman Empire?
10. (a) Which Frankish leader turned Roman Gaul into 'France, the most vigorous of the new nations', and how did he do it?
    (b) In what year and at what age did he succeed his father as tribal chief?
11. For what reason did those German tribes who accepted Christianity choose to follow Arian rather than 'Catholic' teaching?
12. What event in the year 496 was described by one Church historian as 'the most important event in European history', and why did he so describe it?

DISCUSSION AND RESEARCH

13. (If you have Vol. 1 of this course, read pp. 126–129 before answering this question.)
    (a) What event caused Romans to say that their pagan gods protected the city better than the God of the Christians?

(b) Do you think the Romans were right in saying that? Does God protect the cities of Christians in war, rather than those of people of other religions? Give examples to support your answer.

14. Give examples, if you can, of any situations today in which tribal or national groups have chosen to follow one particular form of Christianity rather than another. What effect has this had on (a) the development of the Church, (b) relations between Church and State, and (c) relations between Churches, in that area?

15. (a) Compare Clovis's prayer to God, as recorded by Gregory of Tours (p. 8), with Psalm 115.1–11.

(b) If this prayer summarizes Clovis's reasons for becoming a Christian, do you think he was really 'converted'?

(c) If people become Christian for the wrong reason, does it matter? What could put it right?

16. 'The Roman Empire was being replaced by "barbarian" kingdoms' ... was the Christian religion also doomed to be replaced by paganism? (p. 5)

Some historians have compared the decline of the British Empire in our own time to the decline of the ancient Roman Empire. In what chief ways has the decline of the British Empire differed from that of the Roman Empire? What effect, if any, has it had on the strength of the Church? In what countries, if any, has the Christian religion been 'replaced by paganism' as a result? What, if anything, can the Church do about it?

17. 'The Christian religion . . . had brought to the horrors of war a new factor.' (p. 5)

What was that factor, and in what ways, if at all, does it affect the way in which different nations make war today?

CHAPTER 2

Setback in the East:
Rise of Islam and Arab Invasions

CHRISTIANITY AND ISLAM

Christianity and Islam have much in common. Both are world religions of Semitic origins. In both religions people worship the same God.

There are three religions which claim to be world religions, and which at certain times have spread across great areas of the world: Buddhism, Christianity, and Islam. Buddhism began in north-west India six centuries before Christ. Islam began in Arabia six centuries after Christ. Buddhism spread eastwards, and became the most widely practised religion in East Asia. Islam spread east, south, and west, and became strong in parts of two continents: Asia, particularly central and south-western; and Africa, especially the north.

Among the Semitic 'family' of religions, the most notable are the religion of the Jews, and the two which sprang from it, Christianity and Islam.

Jews, Christians, and Muslims may be said to use the same name for God: a word which varies slightly in each of their languages; the Jews in Hebrew use the word *Elohim*; Eastern Christians in Syriac use the word *Alaha*; Muslims in Arabic use the word *Allah*. People of all three religions claim that in using this name they speak of the one, true, God. And to define Him further, all three would say that He is the God of Abraham and of Isaac and of Jacob, the God who spoke through the Hebrew prophets. Muslims even join with Christians in accepting Jesus as one of the prophets, though Christians, while acknowledging the name Prophet for Him in their Scriptures (Luke 7.16; Matt. 21.11), give Him greater names than that.

So there is much which Christians and Muslims share. Such sharing should help, and often has helped, people of the two religions to understand each other.

Yet the title of this chapter is 'Setback in the East', and we shall now study the beginnings of Islam, because the rise of this religion was the cause of the setback which the Christian Church suffered in the seventh century. This was much greater than the setback in the west one century before; it was greater than any other setback in Christianity's two thousand years of history. It was a setback which, in Islam's first century of swift advance, threatened to encircle Christian populations and hinder Christianity's further spread. Many countries of the Christian

11

Roman Empire were permanently lost to Christian rule, including Palestine, scene of our Lord's earthly life, Syria, and other eastern Mediterranean countries where Apostles laboured. And on the North African coast, it included the homes of some of the greatest Fathers of the Early Church, from Tertullian to Augustine. So we must consider the rise of Islam, and first the country where it all began, Arabia.

ARABIA

Arabia seems to have been the original home of all the Semitic peoples. It is a land which is largely desert. Its people are accustomed to a simple, hard, and wandering life, mostly as shepherds; and from the dawn of history they have had to push out to more fertile lands around. And so there emerged the Babylonians, the Assyrians, the Syrians, and also that small band of nomads whose story the Old Testament tells, the Jews.

In the seventh century AD the time had some for another outpouring of surplus population. The virile Arabs of this period, with swift-footed camels and horses as their most prized possessions, found themselves living between two civilizations where life for the city dweller was on a higher level. To the east lay the Persian Empire, to the west the Roman. These were wealthy civilizations which for the last four hundred years had worn down each other's defences by frequent wars.

We have seen that movements of population caused the fall of the western Roman Empire, the population being German tribes, Goths, Vandals, Burgundians, Franks, and Anglo-Saxons (see pp. 4, 7). The movement of the Arabs began in local plundering raids on neighbouring lands. Finding defences few, and victory easy, they pushed further and attacked in greater strength.

Compared with the movement of German tribes, there was one new factor in the east. The Arab tribesmen began to move out from their homeland at a period when they had for the first time come to know themselves one. This unity was not because of birth into a particular family or tribe, but because they were one in a religion of their own choice, which had captured the whole country and brought it to *Islam*, which means 'submission': i.e. submission to the one true God, and to the rule of His Prophet.

It is important to recognize that two events were happening at the same time:
1. a movement of population from a land which could not support them,
2. the rise of a new religion.

The old idea that this Arab invasion of surrounding lands was a war of religion is largely misleading. It was a war of conquest, but not of forcible conversion. Religion gave the invaders a sense of unity and, with it, the confidence of victory. This was the work of one man, Muhammad.

MUHAMMAD (AD 570–632)

Muhammad was born in 570 into a good family which belonged to one of Arabia's leading tribes, in Mecca, one of Arabia's few cities. His father died, leaving the family poor. As a merchant Muhammad managed the affairs of a prosperous woman, Khadijah, and later married her. They had three children, but none of them lived.

Religion in Arabia was a belief in spirits. The people did not make manlike images to worship, but thought of the spirits as inhabiting certain standing stones. Some of the most important of these belonged to Mecca.

In discussing early Christian influences on Arabia in Volume 1 (p. 107), we mentioned the respect given to Christian ascetics who in the fourth century went to live in the desert on Arabia's borders. In the sixth century some Arabs, not Christians, but seeking a deeper religion than spirit-worship, withdrew from ordinary life to seek God in the silence of the desert. They were called *hanifs*.

After the death of his children, Muhammad was restless and dissatisfied. He left his business and wandered in the desert alone, neglecting his bodily needs as the *hanifs* did. He began to hear voices and receive messages. Sometimes he had visions which frightened him, and messages which came in letters of fire. Sometimes, so he believed, the voice was that of the Archangel Gabriel. He came to believe that he was chosen as God's messenger, and began to expect messages from God.

Muhammad returned to the ordinary life of a merchant in Mecca, but talked much to Khadijah and to close friends about the ideas which had been given to him: God as One, the Almighty; the sin of idolatry; the fear of hell; the rewards of the faithful. As we saw, Islam means 'submission', submission to the one true God. This is expressed in the call to prayer which is made five times a day from the minaret of every mosque:

There is no god but God, and Muhammad is the Prophet of God.

It is impossible to doubt the sincerity of Muhammad's sense of call. Only slowly did he become convinced. His conviction remained unshaken through ten years in which most people rejected his teaching. His first converts were his wife and his kinsmen, those who knew him best.

THE MIGRATION (HIJRA) TO MEDINA (622)

The turn of Muhammad's fortunes came in 622, the year of this migration. It was so important that Muslims treat it as Christians treat the year of Christ's birth, and number the years on their calendars from it.

Muhammad and a small band of his followers slipped away from Mecca, sure of a welcome in Yathrib 240 miles to the north. They were received with honour, Muhammad became ruler there, and the city was renamed Medina, '*the* City', meaning the City of the Prophet. Disregarding old tribal divisions, Muhammad welded the people into one religious community::

'You people, hear what I say, and understand.
Know that every Muslim is brother to every other Muslim.
All of you are equals.' (Muhammad, near the end of his life)

Ten years later, when Muhammad died (632), Mecca had acknowledged him, and so had all the tribes of Arabia.

THE ARAB INVASIONS

Under Muhammad's successors (Khalifs) the Arab raids began, which soon became invasion and occupation of surrounding countries. The first territory they attacked was the East Roman (Byzantine) Empire. In 635 the Arabs took Damascus, in 636 all of Syria, in 638 Jerusalem, in 642 Alexandria and all Egypt. By 652 they had advanced against the Persian Empire, and replaced it by an Arab state centred on Bagdad (see p. 73).

In 697 the Arabs took Carthage, the chief city of Roman North African territory. The rock now called Gibraltar (Arabic *Gebel-Tarik*, i.e. 'hill of Tarik') commemorates the General who in 711 landed there with his army from North Africa, and proceeded to conquer Spain in half a year. Spain, at that time, was held by the Western Goths. From Spain the invaders pushed forward into the very heart of France.

Another Arab army had in 717 and 718 been attacking Constantinople. A glance at the map (p. 17) will show the danger to Christendom. But two events saved it from complete encirclement.

1. The first was the Emperor Leo's victory when he saved the Christian capital, and drove the Arab army back over Asia Minor and behind the wall of the Taurus Mountains.

2. The second was the victory of Charles 'Martel' (French for 'the Hammer'), who earned this name by his blow at the battle of Tours in 732. He drove the Arabs out of France and marked their boundary at the Pyrenees.

Yet what a century (632–732) of Arab advance it had been, and what

2.1 When Muhammad died in 632, the Meccans had submitted to his teaching about God, and so had all the tribes of Arabia. (p. 14)
Ceramic tiles from Asia Minor form a plan of the mosque at Mecca, showing the Kaaba or black stone, the chief centre of Muslim worship.

a century of Christian loss! The Arabs had overrun half of the territory which had once been the Christian Roman Empire. Spain would not be assured of return to Christian rule till 1034. For North Africa, Egypt, Palestine, and Syria, there would be no return. Christian geography was permanently changed. The first great loss of territory has never been made good.

CHRISTIAN LOSS THROUGH ARAB INVASION

We denied that this Arab invasion was a war of religion. That is not to say that Arab rule over lands formerly Christian made no difference to religion. We shall illustrate the difference which it made, (1) from Egypt, and (2) from North Africa.

1. The main body of Christians in Egypt is the Church which is called Coptic. The name 'Coptic' is an abbreviation of the Greek name for Egypt, *Aiguptos* (i.e. Gupt, which became Copt). Its liturgy and Bible are in Coptic (i.e. Egyptian), which is otherwise now a dead language. Arabic, the language of the invader, long ago became the spoken language of the whole land. The Coptic Church today is estimated at two to three millions in a population of twelve millions. Through the centuries the disadvantages of being a Christian have caused a steady 'leak' to Islam. The disadvantages have been a heavy poll-tax on non-Muslims, periods of persecution, marriage difficulties (e.g. in order to marry a Muslim one must become a Muslim), and, not least, the annoyance of being treated in one's own land as if one belonged to a foreign minority. In other conditions, even people who are not *fervently* Christian, do remain Christian. Under these conditions many do not.

2. North Africa is different. To talk about a 'leak' is to think of a bucket with a hole in it. But to think of Christianity in North Africa is to think of a bucket from which the bottom dropped out. The Christian population declined in the destructive Vandal period (see p. 4), and declined still further when Justinian's army fought to destroy the Vandals. Here is a description written at that time:

> 'Men were massacred, women and children enslaved; wealth was plundered; the whole country was full of refugees . . . Libyans who survived fled to the cities, or Sicily, or other islands, most people of note to Byzantium.' (Procopius, *History of the Wars*)

Notice that in these disorders, it was people of *colonial* stock, Roman or Greek, who had somewhere to flee to, and who fled. The Berbers, i.e. the people of indigenous African descent, remained. All evidence points to the fact that the Christian Church had only a slight hold upon these, who were the vast majority. And in the later Arab invasion it was this African population remaining who were won over to Islam.

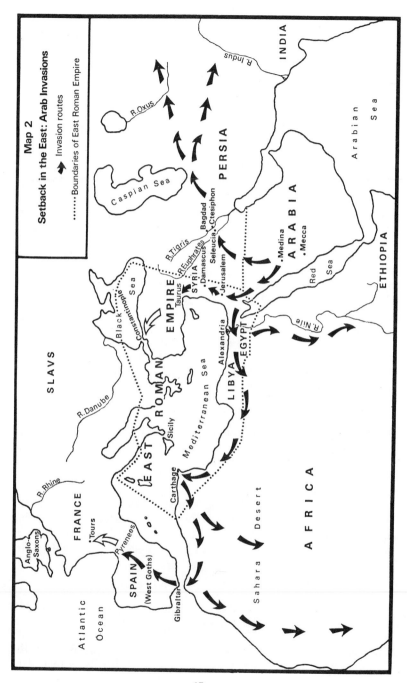

Map 2
Setback in the East: Arab Invasions

➤ Invasion routes
······· Boundaries of East Roman Empire

General Tarik (p. 14), who conquered half Spain for the Arabs in the year 711, was himself a Berber and a convert to Islam. In Augustine's time (he died in 430), the North African coast had 700 bishoprics. By the year 700, the number had shrunk to between 30 and 40. The entire Church in North Africa was soon to disappear.

CHRISTIAN INFLUENCES ON MUHAMMAD

We have seen that Islam, like Christianity, sprang from the religion of the Jews. In going to Medina (p. 14), Muhammad hoped and believed that the large Jewish element in that city's population would join in accepting him as Prophet, and he was disappointed when they did not. The question arises, how much did Muhammad owe to Christian influence?

In Vol. 1, pp. 107–112, we gave an outline of missionary activity in Arabia from about 350 to 525; a 'bishop of the Arabs' mentioned in 364; Churches in the Yemen at Arabia's southern tip; a notable persecution in Najran 300 miles north of Aden in 523; retribution from Christian Ethiopia in 525. The places just mentioned belong to the south, but Arabia was surrounded by possible Christian influences. North-west lay Syria, Palestine, Egypt, all of them parts of the Christian East Roman Empire. To the north-east, the Church of the East was strongest, with its *Catholicos* (Patriarch) at the Persian capital, Seleucia-Ctesiphon. Southward, across the narrow entrance to the Red Sea, lay Ethiopia, which had been a Christian land for three hundred years (since 350).

We are sure of three Christian influences upon Muhammad.

1. First, Muhammad knew the Christians of the Yemen. As the tribes of Arabia made treaties accepting him as Prophet, these Christians were allowed to make their submission to his rule without becoming Muslim. He gave toleration to them, to their property, and to their religion.

2. Second, Muhammad knew the Christians of Ethiopia. Before the Migration to Medina, when his followers in Mecca were being persecuted, he allowed them to seek refuge there, and the Arab refugees were kindly treated. One saying of Muhammad's, preserved in the Koran, refers to this:

'You will find, nearest in love to you who believe,
those who say "We are Christians".
This is because there are priests and monks among them,
and because they are not proud.' (*Koran*, Sura V)

3. Third, Muhammad knew the central place of the Bible in the Christian religion. He classed both Jews and Christians as related to

his own people, because they too were 'People of the Book' (i.e. they had their own Scriptures). His own Book, the Scripture of Islam, the collected sayings of the Prophet, came to be called the *Koran*. This is a Syrian word, used in the Church of the East for the reading of the lesson—a reminder of Christian influences, as well as Jewish ones.

There is also the possibility of Christian influence within Muhammad's own family circle. Zaid, the slave of his wife Khadijah, whom Muhammad adopted as a son, was the child of Christian parents, stolen away by marauding Arabs. It makes one recall what happened when raiding Goths in 264 took Christians as slaves in Asia Minor and carried them over the Black Sea:

> 'These pious captives, by their intercourse with the barbarians, brought over large numbers to the true Faith . . . Of the number of these captives were the ancestors of Ulfilas himself.' (Vol. 1, pp. 121–124)

Ulfilas became missionary-bishop, civilizer of the Goths, and translator of the Bible into their language (341). The Goths brought the Western Roman Empire to its ruin. But the presence of Christians among them was the saving factor—these Christians were the 'remnant' which ensured that the Christian religion would survive (see p. 5).

But the providence of God did not work that way in the Eastern crisis. The influence of 'pious captives' was not repeated there. No translator arose to do for readers of Arabic what Ulfilas did for the Goths. Translation into Arabic dates from the eighth century. There was no Arabic New Testament for earlier Arab enquirers to read.

Christians who saw the rise of this Arab religion recognized its close relation to their own—the same God, the Patriarchs, the Prophets, with Jesus among them; similar practices of prayers, fasting, alms-giving, pilgrimage. They wondered if these two streams might not flow together.

Yet from the start there were Christian customs which caused offence. Christians claimed that Jesus was more than a prophet, was Son of God. This title was, and is, blasphemous in Muslim ears. Christian prayers to God the Father, through the Son, along with high reverence for the Virgin Mary, reminded Muslims of the myths of the heathen rather than the pure monotheism of the Prophets and of Jesus Himself.

As Christians we may well linger over those words of Muhammad about us:

> 'You will find, nearest in love to you,
> those who say "We are Christians".'

That is what they had found in Ethiopia. History would have been different, if, instead of enmity, this sense of kinship had remained and grown. History might have been different if in their own land and language they had been able, from the start, to know the Jesus of the New Testament.

STUDY SUGGESTIONS

WORD STUDY

1. What is the meaning of the word *Islam*, and why is this word used as the name of the religion which Muhammad founded?
2. Who or what were or are:
   (a) Khalifs? (b) Copts? (c) Berbers?

REVIEW OF CONTENT

3. (a) 'Christianity and Islam have much in common.' (p. 11)
   Name two things which they have in common.
   (b) 'Jews, Christians, and Muslims may be said to use the same name for God.' (p. 11)
   What are the names for God used by (i) Jews, (ii) Eastern Christians, and (iii) Muslims?
4. What sort of country is Arabia, and why have its people, throughout history, had to move out into the lands around?
5. (a) What two events were happening in Arabia at the beginning of the seventh century AD, and which of them caused the Arab invasion of lands surrounding Arabia at that time?
   (b) Which of the two events was a 'new factor' which made the movement of Arab tribesmen from their homeland different from the movements of German tribes into the Western Roman Empire?
6. (a) Who was Muhammad?
   (b) In what year and where was he born?
   (c) What was his trade or profession?
7. (a) What sort of religion did Arabs practise before Muhammad's time?
   (b) Who were the *hanifs*, and in what ways were they like some early Christians?
8. What was the *Hijra*, and when did it take place?
9. What two events saved Christendom from being completely encircled by the invading Arab armies?
10. Draw a sketch map to show the countries over-run by the Arab invaders in the hundred years from AD 632 onwards, and mark each country with the year in which it was conquered.
11. (a) What name is given to the Muslim Scripture?
    (b) What is one chief difference between Muslim Scripture and Christian Scripture?

DISCUSSION AND RESEARCH

12. (Before answering this question, find out as much as you can about the life of Muhammad.)
    In what chief ways was Muhammad's life outwardly *like* the life of Jesus, and in what chief ways was it *un*like?

13. What evidence, if any, is there in Muhammad's thinking, of his acquaintance with Christians of his time?
    In what ways, if any, do you think that history might have been different if an Arabic translation of the New Testament had been available in Muhammad's time?

14. What do you understand by the phrase 'Christian geography'?

15. (a) Which countries are under Muslim rule today? Find out, if you can, what is the official attitude of their governments towards people of other religions, and to what extent this differs from their actual treatment of 'religious minorities'.
    (b) Try to find out what attitude towards Christians is taken by Muslims, if there are any, in your own country, and what attitude towards Muslims is taken by Christians.

16. (a) What are the special disadvantages (or advantages) of being a Christian in your own country?
    (b) What, if any, are the special disadvantages of being a Christian in a Muslim country?

CHAPTER 3

The Church and the Anglo-Saxons

We have seen, in the conversion of Clovis, King of the Franks, 'a trivial occasion' which came to be reckoned 'the most important event in European history'.

We now turn to a country which may seem out-of-the-way, but which played a central part in the recovery of the Christian cause in the west—Britain.

Early in the year 598 Gregory I, bishop (Pope) of Rome, wrote to Eulogius, bishop (Patriarch) of Alexandria, telling him of the success of a mission to:

'the *Angles*, set in a distant *angle* of the world.' (Bettenson, *Documents*, pp. 212f)

The Pope liked to play with words, but this word was true. Britain was a distant corner. But it was a corner where a chain of events began which led to the conversion of much of northern Europe. Notice that it is a chain—the events are linked together:

From Britain, heathen Irish raiders carried a Christian boy among their prisoners. He later returned as missionary, *Patrick, Apostle of Ireland, 432.*

From Ireland, which had become Christian, twelve monks sailed eastward under their leader, *Columba, Apostle of Scotland, 563.* Columba died in 597.

From Rome in 597 Pope Gregory I sent forty monks under Augustine—*Augustine, first Archbishop of Canterbury, 597.*

So from both north and south there began the conversion of England.

And then from northern England came the mission of *Willibrord, Apostle of the Netherlands, 690.*

And from southern England came the mission of *Boniface, Apostle of Germany, 718.*

Christians in England, and missionaries from England, played a great part in the conversion of the Northmen, i.e. of Norway, Denmark, and Sweden, conversions well begun by about 1000.

In a period when Islam was destroying so many of Christianity's ancient strongholds—Palestine, Syria, Egypt, North Africa, Spain—

another more northerly line of Christian advance had begun. And surprisingly it had begun from the British Isles.

We shall now review each stage in the progress.

THE CELTIC MISSION:
PATRICK, APOSTLE OF IRELAND (432)

Patrick was a Briton, son of a deacon, who had a farm somewhere on the west coast of Britain. When he was sixteen, Irish raiders carried him to Ireland among their prisoners. After six years as a slave in a pagan land, he escaped and got back home. But he was not left in peace. He dreamed about the Irish whom his Christian faith had begun to influence.

'I saw in the night visions (Daniel 7.13), a man coming from Ireland with letters innumerable. I read one which began, "The voice of the Irish," and as I read, I thought I heard their voice . . . "We ask you, holy boy, come and walk among us once again." ' (Young 42)

Patrick accepted this as the call of God, and after long training returned to Ireland as missionary.

In Trinity College, Dublin, there is Patrick's *Confession* (life-story). The manuscript is a thousand years old, and contains a note to say that it was copied from Patrick's own writing. Its Latin is very poor. Patrick never made up for his lack of books during those six years of slavery. But one book he knew well. His writing is full of remembered words from the Bible, as for example in the passage first quoted, and in that which follows from the end of the *Confession*:

'How is it that in Ireland where they never knew God but worshipped idols . . . there has come to be a people prepared for the Lord? (Luke 1.17) . . . Do not say that it was ignorant I. It was the gift of God. And this is my confession before I die.'

Patrick died in 461.

THE CELTIC MISSION:
COLUMBA, APOSTLE OF SCOTLAND (563)

Columba was great-grandson of the king who ruled Ireland when Patrick was taken as a slave. He was already an abbot, and had founded several monasteries in Ireland, when in 563 'he wished to go on pilgrimage for Christ's sake' (Adamnon), i.e. he felt called to leave, not only his home, but his homeland. From those ready to share his adventure, he chose twelve—a number which shows that his going was not merely a pilgrimage but a mission.

Columba founded a monastery—a cluster of huts made of twigs daubed with mud, with an earthen wall around them—on the tiny island of Iona (map p. 32), and used that as his base. We know of him through Adamnon, Abbot of Iona, who wrote in 690, 'things handed down by our older monks either in writing or by hearing'. Adamnon must have got the account of 'the passing to the Lord of our holy Father' in 597 from the monk who was Columba's personal attendant. When this monk went to chapel for midnight prayers, he found his old master lying before the altar. The account ends:

'His face had flushed with joy when he saw the angels come to fetch him, and so it remained, not like one taken in death, but just left sleeping.' (Adamnon, *Life of Columba* III, 33)

Columba was not only Apostle of Scotland, but founder of the Celtic mission (Celtic means the race of Britons, Irish, Welsh), a mission which, from 635 onwards, converted a large part of England. So the year 597 is the beginning of English Church history, marking the death of the Celtic Columba and the coming of the Roman Augustine.

THE ROMAN MISSION:
POPE GREGORY THE GREAT (590)

Bede, the first English historian, writing in 731, called Pope Gregory I the 'Apostle of England':

'While as Pope he ruled all Christendom . . . it was he who made our nation, then given up to idols, into a Church of Christ. If to others he is not an Apostle, yet he is to us (English) for we are the seal of his Apostleship in the Lord.' (Adaptation of 1 Cor. 9.2: Bede, *Ecclesiastical History of the English People* II, 1)

Gregory I is one of only two Popes called 'the Great', the other being Leo I (440–446: see Vol. 1, p. 143).

Positions of power, whether in Church or State, attract men who love power. But Gregory was not that sort of man. He had been nominated Pope by the clergy and acclaimed by the people of Rome, but he tried to refuse the office. He was born in 540 into a noble family in Rome—then a city of departed glories, much poverty, and danger from barbarian invasions. In 572 he had risen to be governor of the city. Having inherited the family fortune, in 574 he gave it to the poor, turned the great house which had been his home into a monastery of St Andrew, and himself lived the simple life of a monk there. In 578 the Pope sent him as envoy to the Emperor's court at Constantinople, and later used him as his secretary. When called to be Pope in 590 he wrote:

3.1 'Gregory I is one of only two Popes called "the Great". His life had prepared him for the Church's highest office.' (pp. 24, 26,)

A twelfth-century picture from Liège in Belgium shows Gregory in prayer to the Holy Spirit, as seen by the Deacon Peter through a curtain pierced by his pen.

3.2 The carved stone *cathedra* or throne said to have been used by Gregory is now in the church dedicated to him in Rome.

'I wished to be free of this burden, but one cannot resist what God has ordained.'

He must have realized how much in his life had prepared him for the Church's highest office.

Gregory's years at Constantinople had shown him that the Emperor there could do nothing for western Europe. God was calling him to make Rome again to be the place to which men looked for leadership, whether they were descended from the old Roman stock or from the new immigrants, East Goths, West Goths, Burgundians, Franks, and the rest. They would look, not now for an Emperor, but towards the Church which had outlived the Empire. And they would look to himself as Pope: 'Servant of the servants of God'. The most important among his plans was the mission to England.

THE ROMAN MISSION:
AUGUSTINE, FIRST ARCHBISHOP OF
CANTERBURY (597)

The German tribes who settled in Britain, about 450, after the Romans left, are called Anglo-Saxons, a joining together of their two most important tribal names. The Saxons were in the south, and their name still survives in the counties of Sussex, Essex, and the region Wessex (i.e. South, East, and West, Saxons). The Angles settled over a wider area, and so have given their name to the whole Angle-land (England). Why did Pope Gregory send to England, and why to Kent?

The historian Bede tells that Gregory saw fair-haired slaves in the market, remarked (with his well known love of play on words) 'Angles? They have faces of angels,' suggested to the Pope a mission, and offered himself to go. Bede says:

'Directly he was Pope he set his hand to this, sending others in his place.'

In one of his letters, Pope Gregory wrote:

'News has reached us that the people of the English wish and long to be converted to the Christian faith, but priests from nearby do nothing.'

He must have meant the people of Kent, which at this time was the strongest of the several small kingdoms in Britain. Bede writes of its king:

'The powerful Ethelbert's rule extended north to the River Humber. He had heard something of the Christian religion, having a wife of the Frankish royal family.' (*Ecclesiastical History* I, 25)

This queen, Bertha, was great-granddaughter of Clotilda (p. 7). The Pope saw here his opportunity: like her ancestress, Bertha should open the door to the missionaries. Pope Gregory expected much from Christian women in high places. In a coronation service attributed to him there is a bidding to the queen;

'Shun every taint of heresy, maintain your goodness, and call barbarian peoples to the knowledge of the truth.'

That was what Gregory expected Queen Bertha to do, and she did not fail him. He decided to send some forty monks from St Andrew's monastery. To lead them he chose a man of distinction, their Prior (i.e. deputy head) Augustine. Pope Gregory would gladly have gone himself, so the leader was in a special way his representative.

For the forty monks it was a vast and sudden change—from the peace of the monastery to a crowded voyage by ship along the coast, and then the road across Gaul which the Romans had made, but now, alas, without the Roman peace. The Franks, though supposed to be Christians, looked fierce and sounded strange. The Anglo-Saxon language would sound even stranger, and the pagans who spoke it would be fiercer still. They had better go back! So in southern France they halted, and persuaded Augustine to return and ask the Pope to release them from their mission. The Pope replied:

'Better not to have set out on the right way than, having set out, to think of turning back.'

He sent Augustine as their abbot now, who could demand obedience; and gave him letters to bishops and kings whose lands they would cross, and instructions to get Frankish interpreters.

They crossed the Channel just after Easter, landing on the coast of Kent twelve miles east of Canterbury, its capital. From the coast they sent a message to King Ethelbert:

'We bring good news of everlasting joy in heaven, and a Kingdom that knows no end, with the true and living God.'

Ethelbert, not wanting to be shut in with any magic which he believed they might bring, decided to meet them out of doors. Bede says:

'They came carrying a silver cross, and on a board a picture of our Lord and Saviour, singing a litany (i.e. prayers with responses) and praying for themselves and the people to whom they had come.'

The king gave them a house in Canterbury, and they worshipped in St Martin's Church, a small stone church which had survived from Roman times and was used by the queen and her chaplain.

'They preached to as many as they could, accepted nothing more than their food from those whom they taught, and lived as they preached . . . And so *several* believed and were baptized.'

It was a small beginning. Bede continues:

'When, among the rest, the King believed and was baptized . . .'

He implies that, as with the few just mentioned, the king's decision for Christ was a personal one. Ethelbert chose to leave the gods of his fathers for the God of his wife and of these new missionaries. But as a king, his decision made a difference:

'. . . Then greater numbers began to come together to hear the word.'

There was no compulsion:

'Those who prepared the King for baptism had taught him that men must *choose* to serve Christ, not be forced to it.'

And so at Christmas, 597, Augustine was able to report to the Pope that more than ten thousand had been baptized at one time, and the Pope was able to write to his brother-bishop of Alexandria (as we saw at the beginning of this chapter) about the success of this mission for which he had promised to pray. The mass baptism was the result of a mass movement, no longer individuals or heads of families but whole villages and countrysides under their local head-men had been converted. The task of the missionaries was to make the change a real one in the lives of the people.

We know less about what Augustine and his followers did, than about what Pope Gregory advised. His mission policy had two surprising features: (1) far-sighted planning, and (2) adaptation of native customs.

1. FAR-SIGHTED PLANNING

Gregory planned nothing less than the conversion of the whole of England. There would be two 'Provinces', with archbishops at London (soon changed to Canterbury), and York (where, as in the case of London, a bishopric was known to exist as early as 314), with twelve bishops under each (Bettenson, *Documents*, pp. 213f). Such planning is surprising, because there was no 'whole country' to plan for. England was not *one*, but seven or more divided and sometimes warring little kingdoms. Bede says of Archbishop Theodore (668), 'He was the first archbishop whom all the English Church obeyed', and he tells how all the bishops of England met in Council together at Hertford in 673. Only five were present, and a sixth sent a colleague to represent him. Its importance is that it was the *first gathering of any kind* which represented all England (Bettenson, *Documents*, 214–16; Kidd, *Docu-*

ments III, 60–62.) There was an English Church before there was an England, and the far-sighted planning of Pope Gregory the Great began the movement from divided kingdoms to one united nation.

2. ADAPTATION OF NATIVE CUSTOMS

Pope Gregory advised that pagan temples should not be deserted if they could be turned into churches. People would come more readily to accustomed places. He had heard that the English 'have feasts with the sacrifice of many cattle'—meaning the autumn slaughter, due to lack of winter feeding stuffs. His advice was not to stop these feasts but to turn them into Christian festivals (Kidd, *Documents* III, pp. 42f). 'If people are to advance upwards, it must be by steps and strides, not leaps,' he said—the words of a wise and understanding Father-in-God.

Some readers may ask where Pope Gregory got these ideas, and the answer may lie with two other Gregories, both famous missionaries, who lived three hundred years before him. He must have known something of the history of those whose name he bore. The first of them, Gregory the Wonder-worker in Pontus, did turn pagan feasts into Christian festivals (Vol. 1, p. 45), and the second, Gregory the Apostle of Armenia, in a mass conversion took over pagan temples to be consecrated as churches (Vol. 1, p. 90).

Augustine did less than Pope Gregory had hoped, but for seven short years—he died in 604—he did achieve great things. He had converted a king and begun the conversion of his kingdom. He had established a new Province of the Church, with himself as Archbishop, and Bishops of London and of Rochester. And he had linked the island of Britain with the centre of Christendom, Rome, from which he had come.

These were achievements which would endure.

THE CONVERSION OF NORTHUMBRIA: PAULINUS, BISHOP OF YORK (627)

With regard to the northern Province of England for which Pope Gregory had planned, the opportunity came in 625. Edwin, king of Northumbria, was to marry Ethelburga, daughter of Queen Bertha of Kent. Ethelburga was a Christian princess, and one condition of her marriage was that she should take with her a chaplain. Paulinus, who from Rome had joined Augustine's mission in 601, was consecrated bishop to go with her. Like her mother Bertha, and her great-great-grandmother Clotilda, this Christian queen provided the opportunity for the Christian mission.

The Pope, Boniface, gave his support. He wrote to King Edwin:

'This Faith is confessed from east to west, and in his mercy God has begun to warm cold hearts at the world's end, as in Kent.
You know this through your Queen.
Reject idols, their worship, temples, soothsayers.
Accept God, the Father Almighty, Jesus Christ His Son, the Holy Spirit, the life everlasting. For idols are helpless, perishable, man-made.
Accept the Cross, sign of man's redemption. Accept the words of the preachers.
Believe and be baptized, that you may live with God in glory.' (Bede, *E.H.* II, 10 onwards)

This letter is a good sample of missionary preaching. The Pope wrote to the queen:

'Our heart has leapt for joy . . . Your witness has kindled a spark of true religion, which God may turn into a flame of love, in the heart of your husband and the people who are your subjects.'

He sent her, with his blessing, 'a mirror of silver and a gold-mounted ivory comb'.

Edwin considered the question of religion seriously and long, not because he was unwilling, but because he knew that baptism meant a break with all the past and a new beginning. He called together his Witan (i.e. 'wise men', or Council), and consulted them. Bede recorded two replies. The first was a shallow mercenary judgement from Coifi, the pagan high-priest:

'I led in worship of the old gods, and they have done me no good.'

The second is an old counsellor's expression of a deeper need:

'So seems to me, O King, the life of man here on earth,
compared with parts of time beyond our knowledge.
When you are seated at dinner with your lords in winter time,
the hearth-fire in the midst,
there comes a sparrow . . . in at one window, out at another.
For the moment, inside, it is safe from the winter's wind.
But how short its peace, gone in a moment.
from winter to winter, back again out of sight.
So is the life of man. It appears for a space.
What went before, what follows after, who rightly knows?
If this new teaching brings anything more sure, it seems worth following.' (Bede, *E.H.* II, 13)

Sixteen miles east of York is a village now called Goodmonham. The name is Anglo-Saxon, altered to fit modern English. It is really Godmundingaham which means 'homes under the protection of the gods', and the village was given this name because there was a great temple there to Woden, chief of the gods. Coifi mounted the king's own horse, galloped to the temple door, threw in his spear, and called on the people to set it on fire. Bede adds:

> 'The King built a wooden church while he was being prepared for baptism, and in this city of York granted to his teacher, Paulinus, his episcopal See. And so Edwin, with all the nobles, and many of his people, came to baptism in the year 627.'

This was the beginning of York Minster, and not only of York diocese, but (so it was hoped) of the northern Province of Britain which Pope Gregory had planned.

For the mass of the people the font was the local river. Bede says of one place:

> 'For thirty-six days Paulinus did nothing from morning till night but teach people who flocked from every village, and then wash them in the river near by.' (Bede, *E.H.* II, 15)

Crowds gathered everywhere. Paulinus and his helpers were hard at work trying to ensure a Christian future for Northumbria.

But in 633, Edwin was killed in battle against Penda, the pagan king of Mercia to the south. Queen Ethelburga and her children returned by sea to Kent, and Bishop Paulinus with them. It was monks of the Celtic mission who saved the Christian cause in Northumbria.

THE CONVERSION OF NORTHUMBRIA: AIDAN, BISHOP OF LINDISFARNE (635)

Oswald, son of Edwin's predecessor, had kept clear of Northumbria during Edwin's reign. He went north, and among the Scots he found not only a refuge but a religion—he was baptized in Iona. In 635 he returned 'a man beloved of God, with an army small in numbers but strong in Christian faith' (Bede, *E.H.* III, 1). Oswald won the battle, drove out the pagan invaders, and sent to Iona for a missionary. The first one soon returned to report his failure: 'The English are uncivilized, hard and barbarous.' One monk who heard him said: 'Brother, it seems to me you were too harsh. You should have followed the Apostles and given them the milk of simple teaching.' That was why the senior monks chose him to go instead. His name was Aidan.

King Oswald gave Aidan the island of Lindisfarne (map 3A, p. 32), not York, which had been Paulinus's see. Like Iona, it was three miles long, but—unlike Iona in this—at ebb tide one can walk over the wet sands from Lindisfarne to the mainland. Five miles to the south lay

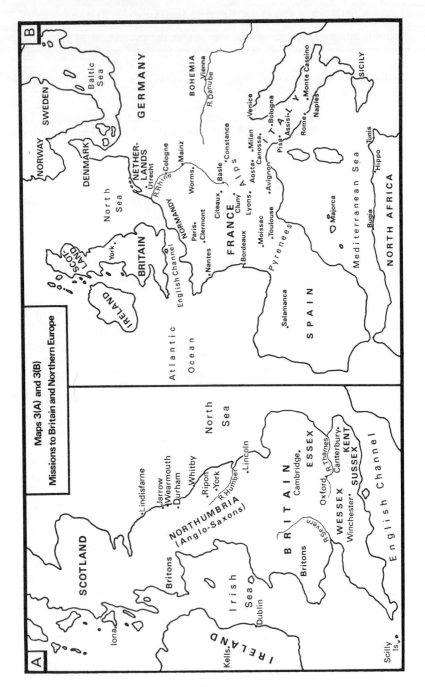

B

NORWAY
SWEDEN
Baltic Sea
DENMARK
GERMANY
NETHER-LANDS
Utrecht
Cologne
R.Rhine
Mainz
Worms.
BOHEMIA
Vienna
R.Danube
Basle
Constance
Alps
Milan
Venice
Bologna
Assisi
Aosta
Canossa
Monte Cassino
Rome
Naples
SICILY
Pisa
Avignon
Citeaux
Cluny
Lyons.
Moissac
Toulouse
Pyrenees
Bordeaux
Clermont
Paris.
Nantes
FRANCE
NORMANDY
English Channel
BRITAIN
York.
SCOT-LAND
IRELAND
North Sea
Atlantic Ocean
SPAIN
Salamanca
Majorca
Bugia
Tunis
Hippo
Mediterranean Sea
NORTH AFRICA

Maps 3(A) and 3(B)
Missions to Britain and Northern Europe

A

SCOTLAND
Iona.
Kells.
IRELAND
Dublin
Irish Sea
Britons
Lindisfarne
Jarrow
Wearmouth
Durham
Whitby
Ripon
York
R.Humber
Lincoln
NORTHUMBRIA
(Anglo-Saxons)
BRITAIN
Britons
Cambridge.
ESSEX
Oxford
R.Thames
Canterbury.
KENT
WESSEX
SUSSEX
Winchester.
R.Severn
English Channel
North Sea
Scilly Is.

Bamburgh, the king's chief residence and fortress. So it was separate, as a monastery should be, yet close at hand to this king who, Bede says:

'humbly and willingly gave heed, and was diligent to build up and extend the Church in his Kingdom.' (Bede *E.H.* III, 3)

Aidan began to preach even before he had learned English.

'Often one could see the lovely sight of the missionary preaching and the king acting as interpreter. For he had learned the language of the Scots . . .

'Then more missionaries came, and so churches were built for different places. People came flocking to hear. The king gave land for founding monasteries, and both little children and those older were trained there.'

Bede gives a vivid picture of the monks as travelling evangelists:

'Bishop Aidan's custom was to travel, not on horseback but on foot, so that, meeting any one, rich or poor, he could turn aside. Did they not yet believe? He would invite them to think of Christian baptism. Were they believers? Then he would encourage them by word and example.

And all who travelled with him, whether clerical or lay, he would make to meditate—I mean either read the Bible or learn the Psalms. This was his daily task and that of all his company wherever they went.'

Aidan belonged to the Celtic mission, but Bede, later on, was brought up in Roman ways. So Bede's praise of Bishop Aidan is the more impressive:

'As a true historian, I have given a straightforward account of the man and his work . . . He was zealous to teach and to do God's will. He knew how to study, and to keep his times of prayer. With true priestly authority he could rebuke the proud and powerful, and with mercy comfort the weak, and relieve and defend the poor. Those who knew him tell us that he took what was taught by the Gospels, the Epistles, and the Books of the Prophets, and did his utmost to fulfil them all. These things in him I much admire and love, as surely well-pleasing to God.'

THE SYNOD OF WHITBY (664)

The presence of two Christian traditions, one Celtic and the other Roman, caused confusion, especially in Northumbria. The king,

Oswy, kept Easter according to the Celtic calendar, while his queen, Eanfled, daughter of Ethelburga, and so brought up in Kent (see p. 29), followed the reformed calendar which was used in Rome.

'When the King was celebrating Easter, the Queen and her party were only at Palm Sunday.' (Kidd, *Documents* III, pp. 52–58)

So Oswy called for a Synod, and it met at Whitby. The decisive speech was from Wilfrid, abbot of Ripon, a convinced follower of Roman ways:

'Easter as we keep it, we have seen in Rome, where the Apostles Peter and Paul lived, taught, suffered, and are buried. So also, in Gaul, where we have travelled . . . And so in Africa, Asia, Egypt, Greece, and all the world, except only for Irish, and Picts and Britons—two distant islands, and not even the whole of them, stupidly opposing the whole world.'

Wilfrid later mentioned St Peter again, 'To whom the Lord said, I will give you the keys of the kingdom of heaven' (Matt. 16.19). King Oswy, more than half persuaded by his wife already, clinched the argument:

'If he be doorkeeper, then I tell you straight,
I am not for setting my word against his.'

Wilfrid's demand was that the English Church should choose the wider relationship and follow the Roman way. We may compare the situation with what sometimes happens today, when a Church growing up to independence, chafes against the narrow denominational ideas of the parent mission, and demands wider, ecumenical relations.

The victory of the Roman party was a sad blow for the Celtic mission, and its monks went back to Ireland. But their influence remained, as we shall see, e.g. in the strong, typically Celtic, missionary spirit of Willibrord (p. 35). The Church in England had chosen the main stream of the Church's life. The choice was good for England, and good for the whole Church, preventing more serious divisions.

WILLIBRORD, APOSTLE OF THE NETHERLANDS
(690)

Willibrord's biographer says that in 678:

'Wilfrid, on his way to Rome, by strong winds was driven ashore in the Netherlands. He was the first to begin missionary work there, a task later fulfilled by that most reverend Bishop, Willibrord.' (Alcuin, *Life of Willibrord*)

In that same year, 678, Willibrord had gone from Wilfrid's monastery at Ripon, in the opposite direction—to Ireland, home of the Celtic mission. There he became disciple of Egbert, a Northumbrian monk who had renounced his homeland for Christ's sake, and was now an abbot famous for holiness and learning. Egbert later began to realize that, instead of Christian Ireland, the place of his 'pilgrimage' (see p. 34) ought to be among the pagans: 'the work of an apostle to those natives in Germany from whom the Anglo-Saxons are known to have sprung'. It is strange that both Willibrord's former abbot, and his abbot in Ireland, should influence him in the same direction. Egbert planned and prepared, and then realized that the task was not for him but for Willibrord. So in 690 Willibrord sailed with eleven others. Alcuin, his kinsman, gives a picture of him:

'Bright with every excellence, well proportioned in body, honourable in appearance, handsome of face, glad of heart, wise in counsel, delightful in conversation, composed in manner, and strenuous in all the work of God.'

Willibrord centred his work in Utrecht. He was the Apostle of the Netherlands, and is that country's patron saint.

BONIFACE, APOSTLE OF GERMANY (718)

Boniface (whose English name was Winfrith) was born in 679, educated in a monastery near Winchester, and chose to stay on there and teach. He became a monk, and was expected to be appointed abbot. But he felt called to share Willibrord's adventures, and joined him in 718, later pushing eastwards into Germany. He was consecrated bishop by the Pope himself (Kidd, *Documents* III, 64–68), who in 739 wrote to praise him for '100,000 German people loosed from pagan bonds'. The expansion of the Frankish Empire under Charles Martel opened Saxony to missionary work. Boniface sent an appeal to England:

'To all who fear God: Remember us in your prayers for this people. Pity them, for their cry is "We are of one blood with you".'

There were regular prayers for his work in many English monasteries and nunneries. Letters and books were sent out to him. And a stream of *hundreds*, both men and women, went as recruits for his mission.

The most dramatic incident in his missionary work was at the Oak of Thor, at Geismar. The tree, like worship of the thunder-god himself, was deep rooted in the past. Boniface said it should be cut down, but who would dare? He would. The crowd watched, expecting that lightning would consume him. Instead, his axe must have struck some hidden weakness. There came a sudden wind, and the great tree crashed down. Boniface called workmen to shape the timbers and from the pagan oak built a Christian chapel—a sign of the passing of paganism in central Germany.

The Pope commissioned Boniface to reform the Church, and as archbishop of Mainz he ruled it throughout Germany. At the age of seventy-five he retired—not to rest, but to return to the simple missionary work with which he had begun. After a preaching tour, he had arranged for his converts to gather for confirmation, when armed men attacked his camp. Boniface called to his followers not to defend him. Long afterwards an old woman told that, as a girl, she had been waiting to be confirmed and saw the old bishop lift up his book to guard his head as a sword came crashing down. Among the relics of the Apostle of Germany there is a blood-stained book, with a sword-cut deep through 140 parchment pages. Some historians have called it a Gospel, but they are wrong. The book contains writings of St Ambrose (died 397) which fit the occasion. One is *About the Holy Spirit*, and the other *How Good it is to Die*. It was Whitsun Eve, and Boniface was reading the first in order to be ready for the Confirmations. He was seventy-five, and was reading the second also in order to be ready for death.

NORWAY, DENMARK, SWEDEN

For the wild Northmen, who from just before 800 onwards raided the coasts of northern Europe, monasteries provided the easiest plunder. They had altar plate of silver and gold, shrines full of treasure, and only a handful of unarmed monks to look after them. So monasteries were robbed and burned—Aidan's Lindisfarne in 793, Bede's Jarrow in 794, Columba's Iona in 795, and monasteries round Ireland's shores. In 851 three hundred of the Northmen's long-boats brought an army to the Thames, and Canterbury and London went up in flames.

But there was a raid as late as 994 which had a different ending. A gigantic Northman, Olaf Trygveson, sailed to Britain intending to rob and kill. But he met a Christian hermit in the Scilly Isles, who told him his fate:

'You will become King of Norway and lead many to the Christian faith. First you will meet an enemy in battle, be sore wounded, and carried on a shield back to your ship to die. After seven nights you will recover. Then you will be baptized.'

Olaf Trygveson fought, he fell, he nearly died. He prayed to the God of the Christians. On the seventh night he felt his strength returning. In the morning he called for a priest and asked to be made a Christian. Then he sailed to England, not to burn churches, but for the Bishop of Winchester to confirm him.

In 995 Olaf became Norway's first Christian King—his kingdom including Iceland and Greenland too. We all have to start the Christian life just where we are when the Gospel finds us. It found Olaf Trygveson, a violent man, and he did not advance very far. But as king he used his sword on behalf of the Christian faith, not against it. He brought over English missionaries to Norway, and some of them crossed into Sweden. Denmark also owed much to priests from England.

From this unexpected source came the conversion of all northern Europe.

STUDY SUGGESTIONS

WORD STUDY

1. What is the meaning of the word 'Celtic' as used in this chapter?
2. Who or what were the following?
   (a) Angles   (b) Witan   (c) Iona   (d) Bede   (e) Coifi

REVIEW OF CONTENT

3. To which country did each of the following go as missionary and become founder of the Church there?
   (a) Columba   (b) Willibrord   (c) Patrick   (d) Boniface   (e) Augustine
4. (a) Retell in your own words Patrick's story of his 'call' to be a missionary.
   (b) What is the chief source of our knowledge about Patrick?
5. Which two Popes have been called 'the Great'?
6. What sort of life did Pope Gregory I lead before he was made Pope?
7. Why did Pope Gregory I send a mission to England, and why especially to Kent?
8. What was the connection between Queen Clotilda, wife of Clovis, and Queen Bertha, wife of Ethelbert, and what did they have in common?
9. Retell in your own words the story of the mission which Pope Gregory I sent to England under the leadership of Augustine.
10. 'Pope Gregory I advised that pagan temples should not be destroyed if they could be turned into churches.' (p. 29)
    (a) Where did Pope Gregory get such ideas?
    (b) Compare Pope Gregory's purpose and methods with regard to traditional pagan customs with those of the Roman emperor Justinian.
11. Who was responsible for taking Christianity to northern Britain (Northumbria), and in which city was he granted his episcopal see?

12. (a) For what reason was Aidan chosen as a missionary by his fellow monks?
(b) Describe Aidan's missionary method and Bede's reasons for praising him.
13. What do Iona and Lindisfarne have in common, and what are some differences between them?
14. (a) For what chief purpose and in what year was the Synod of Whitby held?
(b) What was the outcome of the Synod?
15. (a) Who was the 'Apostle of the Netherlands' and when did he first go there?
(b) What sort of man was he, according to his kinsman Alcuin?
(c) Where did he base his work?
16. What political event opened Germany to missionary expansion?
17. Describe in your own words:
(a) How Boniface demonstrated the fall of the pagan god Thor;
(b) What happened to Boniface in his old age when armed men attacked his camp during a preaching tour?
18. (a) What was the chief object of the Northmen who raided England just before the year 800?
(b) From which countries did the Northmen come?
19. Who was Olaf Trygveson, and what caused him to be baptized?

DISCUSSION AND RESEARCH

20. 'Positions of power, whether in Church or State, attract men who love power.' (p. 24)
(a) What is your opinion of this statement?
(b) Do you think that people who love power are always those best fitted to exercise it?
(c) Do you think that those who hold important positions in the Church are always those who actually exercise the greatest power in the Church?
Give examples from history or from the world today in support of your answers.
21. 'At Christmas 597 . . . more than 10,000 had been baptized . . . the mass baptism was the result of a mass movement.'
Find out whether there have been any mass baptisms in recent years in the Churches of your own or neighbouring countries, and if so, how they came about. Was there a specially planned mission or a revival movement? Did they follow changes of religious or political allegiance within the nation as a whole? Do people in your country normally act as groups in important matters, rather than as individuals? What are the dangers, if any, in mass conversion? How can

mass conversions be followed up and made real in the smaller circle of the family, or with separate individuals?

22. In Question 10 above we compared the purpose and methods of Pope Gregory I regarding pagan customs with those of the Emperor Justinian. Which were the more successful? Compare them now with the purposes and methods of Churches in your own country. How successful have these Churches been in achieving their purpose?

23. We have seen in this Guide that some pagan leaders became Christians because they believed that God had saved them or would give them victory in battle. The author comments: 'We all have to start the Christian life just where we are when God finds us.'
What is your opinion? Give your reasons, and examples to support your answer.

24. Patrick, Columba, Willibrord, and Boniface have been called the 'Apostles' of the various countries where they went as missionaries and founded the Church.
Find out who, if anyone, can be called 'Apostles' of the following countries; and say where you obtained the information:
Malawi   India   Nigeria   Japan   Kenya   Samoa

25. (a) Who founded the Church in your own country, and what records are there of his or their work?
(b) What was the attitude of the rulers of your country to those who first brought the Christian religion, and in what ways has it affected the development of the Church there?

CHAPTER 4

The Church of the East
reaches China

In the year 1625 Chinese workmen, at or near Ch'ang-an, in north-west China, dug up a slab of granite nine feet high and just over three feet wide. It was covered with writing carved in the stone. Beneath a tiny cross only three inches high, was a beautifully written title of nine Chinese characters, *Ta Ch'in Ching Chiao Lau Hang Chung-Kuo Pi'*, i.e. 'Monument of the Syrian Illustrious Religion's Coming to China' (J. Foster, *Nestorian Monument and Hymn* and *The Church of the T'ang Dynasty*, see p. xiv).

The monument was set up in the year 781, and this 'Illustrious' (i.e. light-bringing) religion was Christianity. The date of its coming is given as 635. It is difficult to think of any other early Christian inscription which is so impressive. It contains nearly two thousand characters, and gives (1) a summary of Christian doctrine, (2) a description of the missionaries' arrival, and (3) an account of the fortunes of the Church from 635 to 781. We will change the order and consider the missionaries first.

THE ARRIVAL OF THE MISSIONARIES

The first paragraph of this part of the inscription is in praise of the reigning Emperor, one of the founders of the T'ang dynasty:

'The Way (*Tao*) without a Sage will not flourish.
The Sage without a Way will not be great.
When the Way and the Sage are matched together,
all under heaven are cultured and enlightened.'

Tao (Way) is one of the greatest words in the Chinese language, used in each of China's three religions. In Confucianism 'way' means 'the moral order'. In Taoism it means 'the first cause'. In Buddhism it means the 'path' to blessedness. As Christians we may recall that 'the Way' is the earliest name for our own religion, before its followers were called 'Christians' (Acts 9.2–11.26). 'Sage' is a title given to great men who are also the wisest or most learned—here, to the Emperor. The meaning of the above four lines is that a great Emperor provided the opportunity for a great religion.

It was indeed so. China's influence under the T'ang dynasty reached

40

across Central Asia to the Persian frontier. The Emperor encouraged a revival of learning, invited learned men to his court, and founded a library of 200,000 books (see below). His capital, Ch'ang-an, was the biggest and most prosperous city in the whole world, and ambassadors, merchants, scholars, the sons of kings and nobles, came there from many smaller states. Among such fellow travellers came the Christian missionaries, with good hopes of Chinese interest in the new knowledge which they brought.

This section of the inscription continues:

'There was in Persia a Lofty Virtue (Bishop) named A-lo-pen . . . He brought the true Scriptures . . . rode through hardship and danger, and in the ninth year of Cheng-Kuan (AD 635), arrived at Ch'ang-an . . . The Emperor received him as guest in the Palace. The Scriptures were translated in the Library, and their doctrine was examined in his private apartments. The Emperor, knowing well that it was right and true, permitted its propagation.'

There follows on the inscription a toleration edict which is also recorded in Chinese official documents. It announces the Emperor's gift to Alopen of a monastery in the capital for twenty-one monks.

There is evidence of other monasteries later, perhaps as many as ten. A Chinese record of the year 845 gives the number of monks of the two religions, Christianity and Zoroastrianism (mentioned together because both came to China from Persia), as being three thousand. Clearly this was not just the Church of a small foreign community. There must have been many Chinese Christians.

CHRISTIAN DOCTRINE

From this part of the inscription we can judge whether Christian missionaries, having crossed the whole continent of Asia, had remained true to the original faith, and also whether they were able to express Christian doctrine in so different and difficult a language as Chinese.

(a) GOD

God is one, eternal, inspirer of all Sages.

'There is none but our wondrous Three-One, the true
Lord without beginning, *Alaha*.'

Three-One is of course Trinity, and *Alaha* is the Syriac word for God, similar to *Elohim* (Hebrew) and *Allah* (Arabic).

(b) CREATION

God set the cross to fix the four quarters (i.e. north, south, east, and west), then separated sky and earth, sun and moon, day and night, and made man.

> 'White and clean was his heart, at first without desire . . .
> Then Satan set forth his guile . . . As darkness gathered,
> men lost their way.'

Then follow three most important sections, about Christ. (The word 'Christ' is from Greek: the inscription used Chinese sounds which represent the Syriac word for 'Messiah'.)

(c) INCARNATION

> 'Then one Person of our Three-One became incarnate,
> The illustrious honoured-one, Messiah, hid away his
> true majesty, and came into the world as a man.
> An angel proclaimed the joy.
> A virgin bore a Sage in Syria (Ta Ch'in).
> A bright star was the propitious portent,
> Persians saw its glory, and came to offer gifts.'

This description reflects the ideas about Christ which had been taught by Nestorius (see Vol. 1, p. 141).

In 431, at the Council of Ephesus, Nestorius was condemned as a heretic and deposed from his bishopric of Constantinople. His opponents said that he divided Christ into two persons, one divine and one human. What Nestorius tried to do was to separate the divine and human in Christ when speaking of him. For example, he thought the phrase 'Mary *Mother-of-God*' irreverent. Nestorius himself said:

> 'For the sake of the hidden One,
> I adore Him that appears.
> I separate the natures,
> but I combine the worship.'

Here in the Chinese inscription is a careful two-fold statement about the Incarnation:

First, the *divine* nature:

One Person of our Three-One . . . hid away his true majesty and came into the world as a man. An angel proclaimed the joy. (See Luke 2.9ff.)

Second, the *human* nature:

A virgin bore a Sage in Syria. A bright star was the propitious portent. Persians saw its glory and came to offer gifts. (See Matt. 2.1ff.)

Few Christians today would find heresy in this double statement. The mystery of Christ's person remains a mystery, in whatever way men try to state it. This inscription accepts the mystery and proclaims it.

(d) THE WORK OF CHRIST

'He fulfilled the Old Law as the Twenty-Four Sages had spoken, governing tribes and nation according to great principles.
He established the New Religion of the Holy Spirit from the Trinity, (which is) without speech,
re-fashioning good works according to right-faith.
He determined the salvation of Eight Stages,
refining the earthly and perfecting the heavenly.
He revealed the gate of the Three Constants,
unfolding life and destroying death.'

Here Old Testament religion and New Testament religion are contrasted.

The Jews divide the Scriptures which we call Old Testament, not into thirty-nine books as in our Bible, but into twenty-four, and use the phrase 'The Twenty-four' to mean the Scriptures. The Jewish Twenty-four and the Christian Three-One suggest to the writer of the inscription a comparison which, in Chinese, has almost every word or phrase in the two sentences contrasted. It is difficult to reproduce in English translation.

The Eight Stages are probably the Beatitudes (Matt. 3.3–10).

The three Constants are either Faith, Hope, Love—'constants' because they 'abide' (1 Cor. 13.13); or the three great commandments—'constants' because the Law and the Prophets depend on these (Matt. 22.37—40; 7.12).

Christianity's Three Constants and Eight Stages might have been set out in this way to compare with Chinese Buddhism's Four Noble Truths and Eightfold Path.

(e) DEATH, RESURRECTION, AND ASCENSION

'He hung, a brilliant sun, which scattered the regions of darkness.
The devil's guile, lo, he has utterly cut off.
He rowed mercy's barge, to go up to the courts of light.
The souls of men, lo, he has already saved.
His mighty task once done, at noonday he ascended into heaven.'

'He hung'—this is all that is said in the inscription about how Christ died. In Chinese it was not easy to say. Crucifixion was unknown and the only word for 'cross' in Chinese was, and still is, 'figure ten', which is +. Yet there is no doubt of the importance of the cross to these Christians. The monument begins—even before the title—with a cross, just as, according to the inscription, God ordained the cross, even before creation. (See also (f) below.)

(f) CHRISTIAN CUSTOMS

This part of the inscription ends with a list of Christian customs connected with:

The New Testament:

The Scriptures were left in twenty-seven books.

Baptism and sealing with the cross:

Holy baptism is of water and the Spirit (John 3.5); we hold as our seal the cross which . . . unites all without distinction.

Daily worship; which in the west was called the Canonical Hours (matins, lauds, prime, terce, sext, none, vespers):

Seven times a day we worship and praise, a great protection for the living and the dead. (Compare p. 144, with compline added)

Eucharist:

On one day in seven we sacrifice, to cleanse the heart and regain our purity.

Use of the name 'Illustrious':

The true and eternal Way (Tao) is wonderful and hard to name. Its active energy is clearly manifest.

So it may be called the Illustrious Religion.

THE FORTUNES OF THE CHURCH
(635 to 781)

The Emperor showed his favour by allowing the monastery in the capital to have his portrait copied on one of its walls, 'for ever giving light to the sacred precincts'.
In the years that followed:

'The religion spread through the provinces.
There were monasteries in many cities.
Families flourished in Illustrious (i.e. Christian) blessedness.'

Then in 698 came opposition:

'Buddhists took advantage of their strength, and
raised controversy.'

By the year 712, opposition began in the capital itself. Later, describing the recovery, the inscription says:

'Order was restored . . . The broken net was mended . . .
Altar and sanctuary were repaired. Sacred beams, for a
time in ruins, rose still more sublime. Consecrated stones,
once overthrown, were set back in their place.'

Evidently there had been more than wordy opposition, Christians had
suffered actual violence.

Missionaries from the west, who led in the work of restoration,
were Abbot Lo-han (John) and Bishop Chi-lieh (Gabriel). The latter
is also mentioned in Chinese records as coming to the capital in 732,
with an ambassador from the Muslim Empire which had taken the place
of the the Persian. The bishop had already been in China for some years,
and probably acted as interpreter. It must have been a great advantage
for the persecuted Christians to have one of their bishops getting to
know high officials, and perhaps, along with the Arab ambassador,
being presented to the Emperor himself.

In 742 the Chinese Emperor's favour was restored. He sent a hundred
rolls of silk as his gift to the monastery, and portraits not only of himself but of four of his predecessors for its walls. Another bishop from
the west arrived in 744, and was received with exceptional honour. He,
and seven monks from the monastery, 'were commanded to conduct
worship in the palace'.

The inscription says that in this period the Emperor composed
words, and himself wrote them out, to be copied on to the monastery's
sign-board. In China a man who writes beautifully is as famous as an
artist who paints. The motto over the door of a public building is
often copied from famous writing. However, we have reason to think
that on this occasion the writing was not a motto.

Chinese records include an imperial edict of the year 754, which says:

'The Persian scriptural religion began in Syria (Ta Ch'in).
By preaching and practice it came and long ago spread to
China . . . It is necessary to get back to the original name.
Its *Persian* monasteries shall therefore be changed to
Syrian monasteries . . . throughout the Empire.'

So probably what was copied on to the Christian sign-boards was the
title 'Syrian (Ta Ch'in) Monastery' as written by the Emperor's own
hand in this edict. This edict must have come in answer to a petition
from the Christians. But why should they want to change their name
from 'Persian' to 'Syrian'?

The rise of Islam and the Arab invasion brought loss to Christians
round the eastern end of the Mediterranean and along the North African
coast, i.e. parts of the Roman Empire where Christianity had been the
state religion. Now they were ruled by Muslims. The situation was

different in the Persian Empire. There Christians had been a minority under Zoroastrian rule. With Arab invasion, Persia ceased to be. Zoroastrianism, Persia's state religion, faded away, and Islam took its place. By the period which we are now considering, 745, the new Muslim Empire, under its Khalif (i.e. 'Successor', meaning Successor to Muhammad), was centred upon what had been Persian territory (see map 2, p. 17). Muslims in their newly won Empire were advancing in every kind of knowledge. They had brought little with them from the land of their origin, Arabia. On Persian territory they had come into touch with Christians, who had, through their religion, inherited much of the learning of the Greeks, medicine, mathematics, astronomy, philosophy, art. Such Christians were in positions of trust and influence, and so acted as the teachers of their conquerors—with such good effect that by the year 850 the Muslim Empire became not only the chief Great Power, but the leading civilization.

'SYRIAN' CHRISTIANS

The first Christian missionaries in China had come from Persia, and reinforcements (according to the inscription) continued to come from that same area. It is easy to imagine how impatient they must have felt to be still called 'Persian Christians' in China. Nor would Chinese Christians want to continue such a name. It was common knowledge that the last Persian Emperor had fled from the Arab invaders and had become a pensioner at the Chinese capital in 677, and that his son had failed to recover the throne and died in Ch'ang-an in 707. No Christian wanted a name which would link him to the Persia which had ceased to be. So it was right to name their religion as coming from the land where Jesus was born. That is what the 745 edict says. The 'religion began in Syria. . . . It is necessary to get back to the original name'; *Syrian* Christians they were. They were full of confidence. Persecution was ended, the favour of Emperors restored, and the influence of Christians growing. These lines in the inscription show what they hoped that influence might achieve:

'If winds and rain are seasonable,
if the Empire is at peace,
if men are able to act rightly,
if creatures are able to be pure,
if the living are able to prosper,
if the dead are able to rejoice,
if thought produces its answering sound,
and feeling its own sincerity,
—such is the mighty task and active energy of the
influence of our Illustrious (i.e. Christian) religion.'

4.1 The granite 'Monument of the Syrian Illustrious Religion's Coming to China', set up in 781 at Ch'ang-an, is by far the most important relic of the early Church in East Asia.

4.2 A Christian priest sent to China in 980 said that as a result of persecution and disorder, Christianity there was 'extinct' (p. 51). But the Church did survive in East Asia. 'Persian' angels in a sculpture of the thirteenth or fourteenth century are strikingly Mongol in face and dress.

The misfortune of the Church in China was that it came to its period of greatest influence just as the great T'ang dynasty began to lose its power. In 756 a Turkish army under its own general, which had hitherto been serving the Chinese Emperor by guarding the north-west frontier, rebelled, marched on Ch'ang-an, the capital, and took it. Before its fall, the Emperor and court had fled to the west, and here the Emperor resigned the throne in favour of his son. He had reigned for forty-four years, the longest reign of all the dynasty, and one of the most glorious until this miserable end.

The capital was recovered in 757, but fell before a Tibetan invasion in 762, with Emperor and court again in flight. A third crisis arose in 765, this time a threat from Uigur allies. On all these three occasions, the saviour of his country was Duke Kuo Tzu-i. Duke Kuo's name has been known to every schoolboy in China as an example of service to the nation, and of ideal family life. With regard to the nation, not only the duke himself but eight of his sons and seven sons-in-law held high positions of trust under the Emperor. And with regard to family, Kuo is said to have died at the age of eighty-five with descendants numbering three thousand souls.

A GREAT CHRISTIAN FROM BACTRIA

The monument's inscription is concerned with the fortunes of the Church rather than the State, so it does not directly mention the above tragic events of 756, 762, and 765. But it does mention Duke Kuo, because with the duke, who was commander-in-chief of the armies which saved the country, was Izd-buzid, and he was a Christian, son of a priest, from Balkhin Bactria (map 5, p. 88). Of his being a Christian, the inscription says:

'He was a mild man, loving generous deeds. He had heard
the Way (Tao) and was diligent to walk in it.'

Of his military skill it adds:

'He was as claws and teeth to the duke';

and of his service as interpreter and gatherer of information, among people speaking many different Central Asian languages:

'He was as eyes and ears to the armies.'

When Izd-buzid retired from military service, the Emperor gave him many titles of honour, and valuable presents. The Church gave him the name 'our benefactor'.

'He was able to give away his allowances, instead of

keeping them for his family.
He presented crystal, which had been the gift of the
Emperor, and distributed golden carpets,
retirement presents.
Both by repairing monastery buildings, and adding to
churches, he exalted and adorned their galleries and
walls, as fair as pheasants in flight.
Still more did he devote himself to the Illustrious
(i.e. Christian) faith, in love benefiting others.'

Elsewhere on the Monument, Izd-buzid is referred to as 'priest and country-bishop of Ch'ang-an' (country-bishop being a bishop in charge of a rural area near a more important see). After retiring from the Chinese Emperor's service, he evidently gave himself to service of the Church:

'Every year he assembled the monks of four monasteries
for reverent service and proper worship to fulfil the
whole of the fifty days' (i.e. the seven weeks of the Lenten Fast, and
Easter Day).

The inscription, having praised him for his services to the Emperor, and to the duke, for his generosity to the Church in gifts of wealth and buildings, and his zeal for the proper keeping of Easter, reaches the climax of its praise on a simpler note:

'The hungry came and they were fed.
The cold came and they were clothed.
The sick were healed and raised up.
The dead were buried and laid to rest.'

Here are four of the traditional Seven Works of Mercy (see p. 98).

OTHER CHRISTIAN DOCUMENTS

The granite monument at Ch'ang-an is by far the most important relic of the Early Church in China. There are several other writings, not on granite but on paper, which have survived, surprisingly, for twelve hundred years. They were shut away in a mixed mass of documents in a Buddhist monastery called 'the Cave of a Thousand Buddhas' at Tunhuang on China's north-west frontier. The most important of these documents is a piece of yellow paper four and a quarter inches by fourteen and a half inches. On it are written, from right to left, which is the Chinese way:

1. A hymn of eleven rhymed verses, each verse of four lines, 'The Hymn of the Saved to the Three Majesties' (i.e. the Trinity).
2. A list of Honoured Ones:

The Three Persons of the Trinity.
The Twenty-Four Sages (i.e. Old Testament writers, see p. 43).
The Four Evangelists of St Paul,
and other Saints.

3. A list of thirty-five books, out of a total of five hundred and thirty possessed by the Church in Syriac, 'which the monk-bishop Adam obtained by translation', i.e. translated or caused to be translated into Chinese. It is not easy to recognize the titles when, from the original Hebrew or Greek, they have passed through Syriac into Chinese, but the following seven seem to be likely guesses.

(a) The Book of the Heavenly Treasury is the Breviary, i.e. prayers for the Seven Hours daily (see p. 144).
(b) The Book of the Sage means King David, i.e. the Psalms.
(c) A-wan-chu-li-lung is a transliteration into Chinese of the Greek *Euangelion*, i.e. the Gospel.
(d) The Book of Saint Pao-lu is the Epistles of St Paul.
(e) The Three Majesties Praise (see below).
(f) The Book(s) of Mu-shi are the Books of Moses (the Pentateuch).
(g) The Book of I-li-yeh is perhaps Elijah (i.e. perhaps 1 Kings 17 onwards).

The Hymn (1 and 3 (e) above) is hymn number one in the most widely used hymnbook in modern China, and rightly so. One of the most ancient Christian hymns, it is based on the song of the angels 'Glory to God in the highest' (Luke 2.14). This hymn gradually developed into what Greeks of the fourth century called 'the Morning Hymn', and Latin Christians *Gloria in excelsis Deo*, i.e. the 'hymn' 'Glory be to God on high' which is regularly sung today in the service of Holy Communion. It was carried eastwards into Syriac, lengthened in the process, and was brought in Syriac to China, where Adam (or one of his colleagues) put it into beautiful Chinese verse, slightly lengthened again. Here are two verses in English which will give some idea of:

1. the seven words (monosyllables) of each Chinese line, represented in English by seven 'feet' (or beats);
2. the faithfulness to the Syriac, except for slight lengthening;
3. the ability to put the original into good Chinese expression.

Syriac version in English	Chinese version in English
We confess Thee,	We now with one accord do call
	Thy gracious love to mind,
Through the mediator	Praise yonder wondrous bliss which
of our blessings,	light e'en here in this land gave
Jesus Christ,	Messiah, universal Lord,
The Saviour of the	the great and holy Son,
world and the Son	Extended to this world of woe,

of the Highest.	His boundless power to save.
O Lamb	From everlasting King of Life,
Of the living God,	Thou gracious, joyous Lamb,
	Who didst for all endure the pain,
	nor shrank from toil but came
Who takest away the	To free all living creatures
sins of the world,	from the heaped-up load of sin,
Have mercy upon us.	In mercy do Thou save our souls
	and make them free from blame.

The inscription on the Monument, we saw, ended on a confident note. That was in 781. Soon after the year 900, Chinese records cease to mention the Syrian Illustrious Religion. An Arabic writer tells of meeting in the Christian quarter of Baghdad a Christian priest who in 980 had been sent, with five others, to reinforce the mission in China.

'He told me that Christianity was extinct. The Christians had perished. Their Church had been destroyed . . . Finding no one whom he could aid by his ministry, he returned more quickly than he went.'

The reasons for this disaster were: first persecution, then disorder.

PERSECUTION

In 845 a pro-Taoist Emperor decided to suppress non-Chinese religions, including Buddhism. The edict says, 'How can the trivial religions of the west be compared to ours?' He confiscated 4,600 Buddhist monasteries, and compelled 260,500 monks and nuns to return to secular life. The edict mentions also Christian and Zoroastrian monks exceeding 3,000 who were also 'to return to the world lest they confuse the customs of China'. The policy of persecution lasted for only twenty months. Buddhism with its vast resources gradually recovered. The small Christian Church in China may have been permanently weakened.

DISORDER

In this period civil wars were frequent. In 878 we hear of a rebellion which was ruining South China and bringing to an end its sea-borne trade. 'The foreign merchants return westwards in crowds.' In North China the capital was repeatedly in danger. Lack of a stable government there brought an end to peaceful communications across Central Asia. By sea and land the weakened Christian Church was being cut off from the Mother-Church's aid.

STUDY SUGGESTIONS

WORD STUDY

1. '*Tao* is one of the greatest words in the Chinese language' (p. 40).
   (a) How is the Chinese word *Tao* translated in English?

(b) What does it mean, as used in each of China's main religions: Confucianism, Taoism, and Buddhism?

(c) In what two chief ways is this same word used in the Christian religion?

2. (a) Which two of the following are nearest to the true meaning of 'sage'?
master, liege, scholar, wise man, saint, strong man, ruler, dictator, good man.

(b) Which of the following are nearest in meaning to 'dynasty'?
ruling class, directorate, royal family, dictatorship, despotism, ruling family, hierarchy, heredity.

3. How is the word 'cross' translated in Chinese?

REVIEW OF CONTENT

4. (a) Where and in what year was the monument recording Christianity's arrival in China discovered?

(b) How did those who discovered it know that it referred to Christianity?

(c) In what year was the monument set up, and in which year does it say that Christians first came to China?

5. Christianity was brought to China under the T'ang dynasty.
Why was this a good time for the spread of a new religion there?

6. Who was the bishop who brought the Christian Scripture to China, and how did the emperor receive him?

7. The teaching about Christ in the Chinese inscription 'reflects ideas which had been taught by Nestorius' (p. 42).

(a) Who was Nestorius, and what were his ideas about Christ?

(b) Why did the Council of Ephesus in 431 regard these ideas as heretical?

8. What is the probable meaning of the following phrases in the Chinese inscription?

(a) the Twenty-four Sages, (b) the Eight Stages, (c) the Three Constants.

9. (a) About how long did Christians flourish in China before opposition to them became strong?

(b) From whom did the opposition come?

10. (a) Who were Abbot Lo-han and Bishop Chi-lieh?

(b) When did they come to China, and what advantage did they enjoy in helping the persecuted Christians there?

11. (a) Why were Christian and Zoroastrian monks counted together in the Chinese records of the year 845?

(b) Why did Christians in China want to change their name from 'Persian' to 'Syrian'?

12. Describe in your own words the sudden decline of the T'ang dynasty in 756.

13. Why was Duke Kuo important in the history of China?

14. (a) Who was Izd-buzid?

    (b) Why did the Church in China give him the name 'our benefactor'?

    (c) In what special ways was he like those whom Jesus said will be called 'blessed of my Father', according to Matthew 25.31–40?

15. (a) What relics of the early Church in China were found in the 'Cave of a thousand Buddhas'?

    (b) What 'hymn' of praise which the Church uses today has grown out of one of these relics?

16. The inscription on the Chinese monument showed that in 781 Chinese Christians felt confident of the continuing 'influence of our illustrious religion'.

    What happened between that date and the year 980, when a missionary sent from Syria to reinforce the Chinese Church reported that in China 'Christianity was extinct'?

DISCUSSION AND RESEARCH

17. 'A great Emperor provided the opportunity for a great religion' (p. 40).

    Do you think it is always good for the Church to enjoy the favour of rulers or high officials of the State? Give reasons for your answer.

18. Find out the position and strength of the Church in (a) Syria, (b) Persia, and (c) China, today.

19. (a) Has there been any period since the time when the Church was first founded in your country, when Christianity was 'extinct' there?

    If so, what caused its extinction, and how was it brought to life again?

    (b) What, if anything, can a Church do to avoid becoming 'extinct'?

20. Imagine that you are living in AD 2000. What 'monuments' recording the coming of Christianity to your country might it be possible find then?

21. In what ways, if at all, have the doctrines and practices of the Christian Church been expressed in terms of the traditional religion or religions of your country? If this happened, in what ways has it affected (a) the development of the Church, and (b) the relationship between Christians and the followers of those religions?

Chart 1: TIME LINE AD 400-1000

Year (AD)	LATIN CHURCH	GREEK CHURCH	SYRIAN CHURCH
400			
450	432 Patrick, Apostle of Ireland		
500	481 Franks under Clovis take over Gaul 493 Eastern Goths settle in Italy 496 Clovis baptized		
550	533 Vandals destroyed by Justinian 563 Columba, Apostle of Scotland	527–65 Justinian I Emperor at Constantinople 537 The Church of Saint Sophia built	
600	590 Pope Gregory the Great 597 Augustine of Canterbury		
650	627 Paulinus of York Edwin, King of Northumbria baptized 633 Edwin killed in battle 635 Aidan to Lindisfarne 664 Synod of Whitby		635 Alopen from Persia allowed to establish monastery in Chinese capital
700	690 Willibrord, Apostle of Netherlands		698–742 Buddhist opposition to Christianity in China

Year (AD)	LATIN CHURCH	GREEK CHURCH	SYRIAN CHURCH
700			
	718 Boniface, Apostle of Germany		
			742 Chinese Christians regain favour
			745 Chinese name for Christians changed from 'Persian' to 'Syrian'
750	750 'Donation of Constantine'		756 Duke Kuo saves China in civil war
	753 Pepin crowned King of France by the Pope		Izd-buzid 'our benefactor'
			781 Nestorian monument set up in China
800	800 Charlemagne crowned Emperor by the Pope		
850		860 'Ros' raid Constantinople	845 Pro-Taoist Emperor closes Buddhist, Zoroastrian, and Christian monasteries
		Constantine ambassador to Khazars	Disorder and war in China
		862 Constantine and Methodius to Moravia as teachers requested by Rastislav	
		869 Constantine dies: Methodius works on Slav Bible and Liturgy, used by Slav members of Greek Church in Bulgaria	
900			
950		957 Olga, Duchess of Kiev baptized	
		987 Olga's grandson Vladimir chooses Christian religion for his people	
	995 Olaf Trygvason baptized		
1000			

CHAPTER 5

The Franks and the Pope:
The Greek Church and the Slavs

THE POPE OF ROME

When Christians of the persecuted early Church thought of Rome, they did not remember Romulus and Remus, who were believed to have founded this greatest city of the west. Far more important to Christians were St Peter and St Paul, who had 'poured out their teaching and their blood' there (Tertullian, see Vol. 1, p. 58).

After Rome had become Christian, and then been captured by the barbarian Goths, in 410, St Augustine wrote his big book, *The City of God.* In it he contrasted 'the earthly city which shall not be everlasting', with 'the heavenly Jerusalem', which is the Church triumphant (Vol. 1, pp. 126–129).

Leo the Great was Pope in dangerous times, 440–461. Rome was threatened by the Huns in 425, and was sacked by the Vandals in 455. But the Bishop did not only stay in Rome to bewail its fall. He came out boldly to try to save his city and his people. If he had been asked by what authority he did this he would have said that he acted for St Peter.

This same Pope Leo I addressed the people of the city regarding its two Apostles:

'These are they who raised you to such glory that you were made a holy nation, a chosen people, a princely and royal state (1 Peter 2.9), and head of the world through the blessed Peter's holy See, and so attained a wider sway by the worship of God than by earthly glory. For though you were increased by many victories, and extended your rule over land and sea, yet what your toils in war subdued is less than what the peace of Christ has conquered.' (Sermon on 29 June, festival of St Peter and St Paul)

Rome was the centre of a Church which was destined to triumph and to become world-wide.

After Pope Leo I, only one other Pope has been called 'the Great'; Gregory I (590–604). We might say that Gregory the Great partly fulfilled Pope Leo's prophecy. He was responsible for extending the power of the Church over lands which the Roman Empire had never claimed. In chapter 3 we traced a new expansion of the Church which began from Britain. In 690 it had reached to the Netherlands; in 718 to Germany; by 1000 to the lands of the Northmen; Norway, Denmark, Sweden.

Gregory was responsible for this new expansion, not because he had new ideas about the Papacy, but because as a young man he experienced a missionary call, and when he became Pope he was true to this calling (see p. 26). As Pope he put first among his duties the direction of the Church's world mission. That is what English missionaries continued to expect Popes to do. Before Willibrord began work in the Netherlands:

'He hastened to Rome, so that his mission might be with the blessing and licence of Pope Sergius.' (Bede)

In 695 he went to Rome again, to be consecrated as missionary-bishop by the Pope.

Boniface began his work in the same way, by going to Rome for the Pope's commission; and he was later called to Rome again, when:

'The Pope consecrated him publicly in true apostolic fashion with great solemnity (Alcuin).'

These men showed a regard for papal authority which was unusual in most of western Europe at this time, but which was to last on and spread, until it became typical of the Church of the west throughout the Middle Ages.

Pope Leo had spoken in support of these ideas, but Gregory the Great had done more. He had acted upon them, and his example had been remembered. Gregory had established in England a new Province of the Church, with an Archbishop whom he had himself appointed, and English missionaries in the expanding territories of the Franks followed this pattern. They expected the Pope to give them the same interest and direction, and in each area they established a Province of the Church with an archbishop.

The English contributed, not only by starting the missionary expansion, but by emphasizing the Church's unity. They expressed that unity in obedience to the Pope of Rome, and they followed Roman standards of organization, of liturgy (the Gregorian Sacramentary), and of monastic discipline (the Benedictine Rule, see pp. 144-147).

THE FRANKS

The success of this early mission depended on the patronage of the rulers of the Franks. The Pope, in praising Boniface in 739 for '100,000 Germans loosed from pagan bonds' (see p. 35), added: 'by your efforts *and the help of Charles, Prince of the Franks*'. Some Christians today wish that the work of the Church at that time had been kept clear of politics. They wish especially that the Church had not involved itself in armed conquest. But two things should be remembered:

1. The Church cannot escape from connection with the world. Augustine in his *City of God* recognized that 'the colony on earth of the heavenly Jerusalem' (i.e. the Church) is placed within 'the earthly city which shall not be everlasting' (i.e. contemporary society, or the state (see Vol. 1, p. 129). He recognized that the Church has always to make the best it can of the situation.

2. Conditions of the time may influence and induce the missionary call. 'Charles, Prince of the Franks' means Charles Martel (see p. 14). Charles had no deep religious motive behind his campaign of conquest. But he did share the Franks' general idea that in expanding their rule eastwards they were bringing civilization and peace to the lands of their German ancestors. This idea was similar to the missionary motive which we have already noticed, and which does go deep, i.e. as seen in Egbert, abbot to Willibrord in Ireland, who felt called to do:

'the work of an Apostle to those nations in Germany from whom the Anglo-Saxons are known to have sprung' (see p. 35).

It was the same idea which led Boniface to ask that prayers should be offered in English Churches for his missionary work among those who are 'of one blood with you' (see p. 35).

The Pope began by asking Charles Martel in 722 to protect his missionary, Boniface, and Charles promptly issued a safe-conduct:

'He must be preserved quiet and safe in our love, protection, and defence, on this condition, that he does justly.'

Charles Martel was not actually king of the Franks, but mayor (i.e. master) of the palace. Among the Franks the king, who was a descendant of Clovis, had at this time become a mere figurehead, and the mayor of the palace (or as we might say, the prime minister) was the real ruler. Charles probably felt pleased that the Pope realized that the power was in his hands. So he was willing to protect Boniface— but only on condition of his obedience.

Charles Martel sent his two sons, Carloman and Pepin, to be educated by the monks of St Denys's monastery near Paris. There they grew up to be even more deeply devoted than their father, both to the Church, and to the head of the Church in Rome.

Charles Martel died in 741, and Carloman and Pepin became joint mayors of the palace. But in 747 Carloman felt called to the life of religion, and became a Benedictine monk at the great monastery at Monte Cassino.

Thus Pepin became sole ruler. 'To me,' he said, 'the Lord has entrusted the care of the government.' The Pope had at this time turned Boniface from pioneer missionary work, and had made him archbishop of Mainz in 747, with the task of reorganizing and reforming the Church throughout Germany. Pepin zealously supported Archbishop Boniface in strengthening the Church. He established new provinces, each under its archbishop; appointed many new bishops; and encouraged better clergy, stricter discipline, and annual synods. Pepin himself said:

'If God grant us peace, we hope to get back to the standards of the saints (i.e. of the Early Church).'

Pepin must have done much to provide for the needs of the mission. In a letter of the year 752, the aging Boniface pleaded for continued support for his many missionaries—priests, monks, and nuns—after his own death, adding 'almost all of them are foreign'. And later he wrote;

'May the Lord Jesus give you an eternal reward in heaven. You have comforted my old age and infirmity.'

As for relationships with the Pope, there was a difficulty. Nominally Rome lay within the continuing Roman Empire, which was now ruled from Constantinople. But since Gregory I's time Popes had acted like independent rulers of the city of Rome and of territory around it, i.e. the Duchy of Rome. And by Pope Gregory III's time (731–741), they had even broken off political relations with the Emperor. However, the Pope and his territories needed a protector. Gregory III had recognized this, and had turned to Charles Martel as the only one who might strike a blow against the Lombards on his behalf (map 4, p. 69).

Charles had hesitated to interfere in Italy, but not so Pepin, his son. Pepin made known his readiness by sending envoys to the Pope with a simple question: Was it right that one man (Clovis's descendant) should bear the name of king, while another (himself) should bear responsibility of rule? The Pope replied that this was not right. This reply was reported to the assembly of Frankish nobles, who then declared Clovis's descendant deposed, and elected Pepin as king. But that was not all. Pepin was anointed king, as David was in 1 Samuel 16.13, and was declared 'king by the grace of God'. It seems likely that Archbishop Boniface did the anointing. In 753 the Pope himself came north to Paris. At the monastery of St Denys, where Pepin had gone to school the Pope crowned him 'king of the Franks and patrician of the Romans' (i.e. of the Roman nobility). This title showed where the Pope now looked for protection.

Here was something new: the Pope had decided that a king should be deposed, and that another should be made king, and had himself crowned him. King Pepin, as he now was, soon afterwards crossed the Alps into Italy, and recovered lands which the Lombards had invaded.

Then, instead of returning them to the Emperor, he added them to the territory of which the Pope was ruler. The ruler of the Franks and the Pope of Rome were advancing in their claims of power, and they were advancing together.

CHARLEMAGNE

King Pepin died in 768, and was succeeded by his son Charles, who is usually known as 'Charlemagne' (*magne* comes from the Latin *magnus*, 'the Great'). He is rightly called 'great'. He was a great warrior, who doubled the size of the kingdom he received from his father (map 4, p. 69). He was also a good organizer, and did much to improve the government of State and Church, keeping a firm hand on both.

Charlemagne was a patron of learning, though not learned himself. He never learned to write, and he read Latin with such difficulty that he preferred to have some one read to him. But he respected learning and encouraged it. He liked to have learned men around him, and was wise in his choice of them. For example, he met in Italy Alcuin, head of the cathedral school at York. This school was founded by a pupil of Bede, the first learned Englishman (see p. 24).

Alcuin was a kinsman of Willibrord, and wrote his life. Charlemagne invited Alcuin to be head of his palace school and adviser on education in his kingdom. With the coming of Alcuin a light begins to shine in Europe's Dark Ages. After the death of Charlemagne the darkness of ignorance again descended. But men did not forget the place which Charlemagne had given to learning, the respect for books and care in copying them which he encouraged, or the central presence of learned men around the king, and the cultural standard he set up in the king-dom. Twelve Latin classics have survived only in the copies made in Alcuin's time.

As a Christian, Charlemagne's own life was further from Christian standards than was his father's, probably because he had grown up among the lax morals of a court, not under the discipline of a monastic school. But his policies as ruler were meant to strengthen and extend the Christian faith, even if some of them were misguided, for example the use he made of the Church in trying to subdue the heathen Saxons:

'He brought together a great army, invoked the name of Christ and set out for Saxony. He took with him a crowd of clergy, abbots, and priests, that they might cause the people to accept the yoke of Christ . . . He converted the greater part of the people, some by the sword, some by persuasion, some through gifts . . . He divided every province into dioceses, and gave the Lord's servants power to teach and to baptize.' (Eigil, *Life of Sturmi, Abbot of Fulda*)

Alcuin protested boldly against the use of force. He wrote to one of Charlemagne's highest officials, 'Let those who teach the Faith be *preachers* not *predators*', and to the king himself:

> Let peace be made with the Saxons, wicked as they may be.
> Let threats be relaxed, so that men's hearts be not hardened.

And to a fellow bishop he expressed himself even more forcefully:

> 'What use is baptism without faith.
> Faith must be voluntary, not forced.
> How can a man be made to believe what he does not believe.
> He might be forced into baptism but not into faith.'

In 773 the king of the Lombards again threatened the Pope's territories, and the Pope, Hadrian, called to his aid 'the patrician of the Romans'. Charlemagne crossed the Alps into Italy with a great army, destroyed the Lombard kingdom utterly, and set Rome free. The young king (he was thirty-two) was welcomed by a grateful Church. It was his first sight of Rome: the tombs of St Peter and St Paul, the relics of the martyrs, the splendid churches, the majestic worship. This was indeed the Holy City, and he would always be its protector.

THE POPE AND THE EMPEROR

Charlemagne, as we saw (p. 60), liked to have books read to him. His favourite was Augustine's *City of God*, one of the biggest books in size, and in importance that had come down from the Early Church (Vol. 1, pp. 127–9). We can imagine Alcuin reading it aloud to him, and the two discussing it (as we know they did) in the light of their own times:

The two cities were:

1. The heavenly Jerusalem, the Church triumphant, which has its colony on earth, the Church militant. And that, Charlemagne would say, centres upon a city, Rome, remembering the glories which he saw there.

2. The earthly city. That, Alcuin would remind him, was the Roman Empire, persecuting the Early Church. Charlemagne remembered the martyrs' tombs in Rome, 'Until the help of God brought those who opposed to a change of mind.' The Christian Empire had indeed given the Church peace. Charlemagne recalled his father's words:

> If God give us peace, we hope to get back to the standards of the saints.

The Church certainly needed a strong State to protect it. The Pope could not protect himself. With regard to worldly power, he ruled a mere dukedom. But Charlemagne ruled an empire which encircled it, and he could, and would, give the Church peace. Alcuin encouraged

5.1 'In God's scheme of things, the Pope of Rome held spiritual power, and the Emperor of Rome held worldly power . . . each needing the other' (p. 63). This idea is expressed symbolically in an eighth-century mosaic in St John Lateran in Rome: St Peter giving the pallium to Pope Leo III, and a battle standard to the Emperor Charlemagne.

5.2 Vladimir's conversion was the beginning of Christianity in Russia. An early fresco shows him with his retinue.

Charlemagne to think that in God's scheme of things, in which the Pope of Rome held spiritual power, and the Emperor of Rome held worldly power, he, Charlemagne, had a part.

Towards the end of his life Charlemagne again came to Rome, for Christmas in the year 800.

'As the King rose from his knees at Mass, the Pope placed a crown upon his head, and the whole Roman people hailed him. "To Charles, be life and victory, crowned of God, great peace-bringing Emperor of the Romans".'

One early record says that 'if he had known of the Pope's intentions, he would not have gone to church that day'. Charles may have felt that, when the Pope needed a protector, he had protected him and his city. In so doing he had acted as Roman Emperor, but it was his own action, not the Pope's crowning, which made him so. Pope and emperor, each needing the other—that situation recurred in the west throughout the Middle Ages. Charlemagne did need the Pope. For after all, 'Emperor of the Romans' was a title which no one but the Pope could give.

THE 'ROS'

By a strange chance, an event of the year 860 first brought to prominence in history: (1) The *Ros*, original form of the word 'Russian, and (2) Constantine and Methodius, two Greek brothers, who later became, for Russians and for the whole Slav race, their greatest missionaries.

Photius, a Greek of noble family, who was the most learned man of the period, and newly made Patriarch of Constantinople, in 860 wrote:

'The Ros, a nation living far away, barbarians and nomads, have suddenly poured over our frontiers, devouring the inhabitants of the land and sparing neither man nor beast.'

These 'Ros' were originally not Slavs but Northmen. They were Swedes from the region of the Baltic Sea (map 4, p. 69), who had pushed southwards across the plains and along rivers. One of their routes was down the river Dnieper to the Black Sea, another down the greater river Volga to the Caspian Sea. Some of them settled among the simpler Slav population of those regions, adopted the Slav language, became defenders of the towns, and so came to be their rulers. The name of this ruling class was gradually accepted by the Slav population too. This was the real beginning of Russia.

Photius was writing about one such community settled around Kiev. They had come down the river Dnieper in more than two hundred boats, crossed the Black Sea, raided Constantinople, and then returned with their loot.

The Emperor saw a new danger here, and decided to try to renew alliance with the Khazars, a Turkish people who lived between the rivers Volga and Don (map 4, p. 69). Among the Khazars the Jewish, Muslim, and Christian religions had all begun to win a following, in that order of success. So Emperor and Patriarch decided to include among their ambassadors someone able to deal with any religious question which might arise. They chose Constantine, a man already distinguished in the Church and also among learned men of the city.

CONSTANTINE AND METHODIUS

Constantine had been private secretary to a previous Patriarch of Constantinople, the ruling bishop of the Greek Church. He had in his student days been taught by Photius, and had succeeded him as a philosopher in Constantinople. He was also a noted linguist. Born in Salonica (Thessalonica of the New Testament) in 826, he grew up speaking not only Greek but the Slav language too, since there was a Slav settlement near. He also learned Semitic languages, all of which he improved in his later travels: Hebrew, Syriac, Samaritan, Arabic. Methodius was his elder brother, a man of outstanding abilities too, but used to working with his brother, and content to take a second place.

Many stories have been recorded which show Constantine's quick humour. For example, among Khazar converts to Judaism, he found some who boasted of their new rank as 'sons of Abraham'; so he remarked that, as a Christian, he could claim to be a grandson of Adam, and thus take precedence.

Once, among Muslims, he heard Christians being reproached for having drawings of devils made on their house-doors, the work of Muslim neighbours. So he suggested that the devil was *outside* the Christian's door, whereas previously he had been resident within.

And when fellow Christians opposed Constantine's own idea of services and scriptures in Slav language, saying that worship could only be in the three languages in which Pilate wrote, 'Jesus of Nazareth, the King of the Jews . . . in Hebrew, in Latin, and in Greek' (John 19.19, 20), Constantine retorted:

Then you are disciples of Pilate, not of Christ.

With this last illustration we pass from Constantine's humour to the task which was to be his life's work: the Christian religion translated into Slav language. That meant, first, devising an alphabet so that the Slav language could be written down. When Constantine suddenly produced such an alphabet ready-made many of the people said it was a miracle. Probably he and Methodius had been working on the idea for years; Methodius had spent some time as governor of a province where many Slavs had settled.

Methodius accompanied Constantine on this journey. They spent the winter at Kherson in the Crimea (map 4, p. 69), where happened one of the greatest events of his life, or so he thought: He discovered what he believed to be the grave of St Clement of Rome (see Vol. 1, p. 63). This introduces us to a subject which was important throughout medieval Christendom, and is still important to many Christians today, so we may mention it in some detail.

We noticed in Volume 1, p. 32, the beginning of Saints' Days, with the martyrdom of Polycarp, bishop of Smyrna, in 156. At his grave, said Christians of Smyrna:

We shall gather with joy and gladness, to celebrate the birthday of his martyrdom.'

We noted that this was the 'first of an ever-increasing number'.

The right and proper remembering of the Church's saints easily degenerated into a too eager collection of holy *things*. In an uncritical age, Christendom was filled with supposed relics, i.e. remains of the saints' bodies, or objects which they had possessed, which people later treated as having a magical power in themselves.

A legend of the fourth century (which is not supported by any direct evidence) said that Clement was arrested and sent to the Crimea to work in the mines, and then martyred by being tied to an anchor and thrown into the Black Sea. Perhaps Constantine discovered at Kherson a gravestone with an anchor carved on it. There are many such carvings, because of Hebrews 6.19;

'A sure and steadfast anchor of the soul, a hope that enters into the inner shrine.'

Whatever its reason, Constantine had no doubt about the grave's being St Clement's. He took away some of the bones, and accepted St Clement as patron of his mission. When later he went to Rome, the Pope came out to meet him, and great crowds gathered, because of the relics which he brought. They were escorted in procession to the Church of St Clement, supposed to be on the site of his former home. Constantine, who died in Rome, was buried there. The remains of a fresco over his grave can still be seen, which shows Constantine at the Last Judgement receiving the Lord's 'Well done'.

As winter passed, the embassy travelled east to meet the ruler of the Khazars on the shores of the Caspian Sea (map 4, p. 69). Evidently there was some discussion of religion, and as a result of Constantine's witness, two hundred people are said to have decided for the Christian faith. Constantine got permission from the ruler, who was himself pro-Jewish, for these of his subjects to be baptized, and also permission for two hundred Greeks, taken prisoner in frontier war, to return home.

With regard to the danger from the Ros, the Khazars did renew the treaty of alliance, saying:

'We are friends of the Empire, and at your service whenever you should call.'

From their share in this successful embassy the two brothers returned: Constantine to his teaching and study of philosophy, Methodius to become abbot of a monastery. And soon their real mission claimed them.

THE MISSION TO MORAVIA

Slav settlers in eastern Europe tended to turn to the Greek Church. For example, Slavs were recruited into the armies of the Eastern Roman Empire, just as Goths had earlier entered those of the Western Roman Empire (p. 4). Since the Empire was Christian and its citizens observed Christian worship and kept the Christian festivals, Slav recruits took part without question. They were accepting the Greek way of life, and accepted the Greek Church as a part of it.

Central Europe was different. The area which today is Czecho-slovakia, Austria, Hungary, and Yugoslavia, had been subdued by Charlemagne and had become Slav provinces of his Empire. The Empire was now divided, and this, its eastern end, was the kingdom of Charlemagne's grandson, Louis, called 'the German'. Both the Latin Church based on Rome, and the Greek Church under the Patriarch of Constantinople, were trying to win these Slavs. Politically they belonged to the west; but they might accept Christianity's eastern form because other Slavs belonged there.

In 862 Rastislav, Prince of Moravia (map 4, p. 69), sent this message to the Emperor at Constantinople:

'Our people have renounced paganism and are observing the Chris-tian law, but we have no teacher to explain to us the true Christian faith in our own language, so that other nations, seeing this, may follow our example. So send us, Sir, such a bishop and teacher.'

The Emperor did not send a bishop, since Moravia was Frankish territory, claimed by the Latin Church. But he did send a teacher, indeed two, Constantine and Methodius.

Missionaries at the eastern end of the Early Church had encouraged use of the various peoples' own languages for scriptures and liturgy (e.g. Syriac, Armenian, Coptic, Gothic, etc.; see Vol. 1, p. 122). During the Dark Ages the idea had become strong in the Church of the West that learning must be expressed in Latin, and that other languages were barbarous and illiterate. With these two Greeks, use of the native tongue was more than a policy, it was a principle. Constantine had already produced his Slav alphabet. He began a translation of the Gospels before leaving Constantinople, choosing first St John's Gospel. One wonders how many translations of the New Testament have begun with this book, which is in simple Greek that can be simply translated. For example, in English translation the first paragraph contains 65 words, of which all but five are monosyllables, as simple as the language of a child's first reading book, yet expressing the very heart of the Gospel (John 1.1–5).

Constantine and Methodius translated the Daily Office (i.e. the ser vices for the Seven Hours—see p. 144), the Gospels, and the liturgy of St John Chrysostom which was the most-used form of the Eucharist in the Greek Church. Along with these they translated a poem (only rediscovered in 1858) appealing to Slavs to accept and treasure literature in their own language. Then to show that, while they discouraged the Latin language they had no prejudice against Latin ways, they produced a Slav version of the Latin Mass.

Despite the disagreement between the Greek and Latin Churches, in 868 they were invited to visit Rome, with a welcome by the Pope and the people of the city for Constantine and for the relics of St Clement (p. 65). The Pope showed his welcome too for the Slav books, receiving them at the altar of the church of St Mary. In the great church of St Peter, men whom Constantine had trained as clergy were ordained by the Pope, and there they sang the liturgy in Slav language, afterwards singing through the night 'in the church of that great teacher of the world, the Apostle Paul'.

In 869, there in Rome, Constantine died, after taking vows as a monk and receiving the monastic name of Cyril. This is the reason for his often being referred to as Cyril, not Constantine. His reason for becoming a monk was this:

'From now on, I am the servant neither of the Emperor nor of any one on earth, but only of God the Almighty.'

He was only forty-two.

His dying wish had been that Methodius should complete their work in Moravia. Methodius did place himself at the disposal of the Pope, and was made bishop and sent back as papal legate to Moravia. It is cheering to find that at this period, when division was increasing, missionaries of the Greek Church were coming to be accepted by the Latin Church, and were being encouraged in the creation of a Slav section within it. It is also pleasing to record that in 881 Methodius visited Constantinople, where he was honoured by the Emperor and the Patriarch. They both showed a lively interest in the Slav Bible, which Methodius had by then completed, and in the Slav liturgy. Methodius died in 885, and, appropriately, his funeral service was in three languages, Latin, Greek, and Slav. He belonged to all three.

THE BENEFIT TO ALL THE SLAVS— AND TO RUSSIA

The work of the two brothers, which began with such notable recognition by the Pope, was later rejected because narrower policies, for the use of Latin only, prevailed in the Church of the West.

But the Bulgarians gave it a second, and a wider, opportunity. In 870, after hesitating between Latin and Greek Churches, their king, Boris, decided for the Greek side. Clergy in Moravia, who had been driven out by reaction against the Slav liturgy, were welcomed in Bulgaria, and here the Christian religion first came to full Slav expression. Indeed that which Rastislav had hoped might happen for his own people, 'that other nations, seeing this (a Slav Church) may follow our example', was fulfilled among the Bulgarians. And so the Church which was centred in Constantinople (or New Rome, as it was called, not the old Rome of the Papacy) was able to win almost all the Slav nations to a religion related to, and as far as literature is concerned basic to, their own culture.

The greatest among such nations was represented by the East Slavs. The Patriarch Photius had sent missionaries to the area around the river Dnieper, and in a letter of 867 he reported that the Ros, 'cruel enemies of Byzantium, were now becoming friends and had accepted a bishop and priests'. Constantine may have rejoiced to hear of this before he left Moravia. However, this early success was not continued.

By the year 950 there were a number of Christians in Kiev (map 4, p. 69), and in 957 Olga, who had succeeded her husband as ruler there, went to Constantinople to be baptized. Olga's son, a pagan, married a lady of her household, who must have been at least a nominal Christian. So Olga's grandson, Vladimir, spent his childhood under mixed influences, half Christian, half pagan. The pagan in him was strengthened by spending part of his youth in Sweden, which was not yet a Christian country. In 978 Vladimir succeeded as ruler of Kiev, with the earth goddess (for fertility), and the war god, Thor, as the powers on whom he depended. But Christian influences increased.

Everyone who writes of Vladimir repeats the story of his sending envoys to neighbouring peoples to examine their religions, and advise him which to follow:

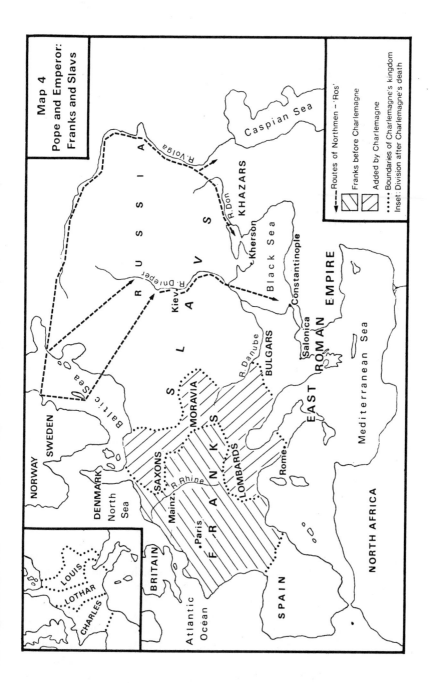

Map 4
Pope and Emperor:
Franks and Slavs

Routes of Northmen - 'Ros'
Franks before Charlemagne
Added by Charlemagne
Boundaries of Charlemagne's kingdom
Inset: Division after Charlemagne's death

Caspian Sea

R.Volga

KHAZARS

R.Don

Kherson

RUSSIA

R.Dnieper

Kiev

SLAVS

Black Sea

Constantinople

EAST ROMAN EMPIRE

Salonica

R.Danube

BULGARS

MORAVIA

SLAVS

Mediterranean Sea

Baltic Sea

SWEDEN

NORWAY

SAXONS

R.Rhine

FRANKS

LOMBARDS

Rome

DENMARK

North Sea

Mainz

Paris

BRITAIN

Atlantic Ocean

SPAIN

NORTH AFRICA

LOUIS

LOTHAR

CHARLES

69

'The Muslims among the Bulgarians stand, bow, sit, look around this way and that, like men possessed. There is no joy in their worship.
We saw the Germans celebrating their Latin service and found no beauty in it.
The Greeks took us to their Church (see p. 3), and we did not know whether we were in heaven or on earth . . .
We only know that their God dwells among men.' (Kidd, *Documents* III, pp. 103-107)

Modern scholars say that the story at least represents Vladimir's possibilities of choice. Had his choice been Islam, how different history would have been!

We may here add that the appeal of Orthodox worship is similarly described by a Japanese boy who experienced Christian worship for the first time in an ordinary chapel of the Russian Church's mission in 1881:

'Not the words of the priest, nor the resounding singing, nor the oft-repeated chant . . . Attention was fixed somewhere far away, invisible to me. I caught the mood, felt at ease, even joyful . . . "If there is a God", I thought, *"He is there".'* (Abbreviated from translation from the Russian)

In about 987 Vladimir had married Anne, the Greek Emperor's sister. He was baptized in 988, and asked for priests from the Church of the East to establish Christianity in his dominions. Monks soon followed and a strong monastic movement spread all over Russia. Naturally the Russian Church took the eastern side in the schism of 1054 which divided the Church in two (p. 131).

Vladimir's conversion was the beginning of Christianity in Russia. And in Russia Christianity was to prove in a quite special way to be the salvation of the nation. The sweep of the Mongols across Asia and into Central Europe in 1238 (see p. 79) almost destroyed Russia. When after two centuries the Russians were free from barbarian domination, they rebuilt their civilization around the Church, which became the symbol of their national unity. Later still, when all the Balkans fell to the Ottoman Turks, the Russian Church remained sole guardian of orthodox Christianity in Europe.

Because of his importance in their history, Russians tried to make Vladimir a saint, and even called him 'equal to the Apostles'. But in behaviour he was not even up to ordinary Christian standards. For Russia and the whole Slav family of peoples, the real saints and apostles are the two Greek brothers, Constantine and Methodius.

STUDY SUGGESTIONS

WORD STUDY

1. Who or what were the following?
   (a) Ros   (b) Khazars   (c) Slavs
2. Alcuin said 'let those who teach the Faith be preachers not predators'. Which of the following words are used for men who have the same or nearly the same task as a 'preacher', which mean the same or nearly the same as a 'predator'?
   preceptor   prelate   pirate   pillager   presbyter   predicator
   peculator   raptor   pastor
3. (a) What does the name *Charlemagne* mean?
   (b) What did Charlemagne do to deserve this name?

REVIEW OF CONTENT

4. Whom did Christians of the early Church think of as bringing greatest glory to the city of Rome, rather than Romulus and Remus its founders, and for what reason?
5. Explain the statement that 'Pope Gregory the Great partly fulfilled Pope Leo the Great's prophecy'. (p. 56)
6. (a) Name two missionaries of the seventh and eighth centuries who went to Rome to obtain the Pope's blessing and commission before starting their work.
   (b) In what other ways did English missionaries at this time show their regard for the Pope's authority?
7. Charles *Martel* got his nickname 'the Hammer' because of his success as a military leader. What other official position did he hold among the Franks?
8. (a) What were the names of Charles Martel's sons?
   (b) What sort of career did each follow?
9. (a) For what reasons did the Papacy need a protector in Pope Gregory III's time?
   (b) Describe the events which led to Pepin's becoming protector of the Papacy.
10. Who was 'the first learned Englishman'?
11. 'With the coming of Alcuin a light begins to shine in Europe's Dark Ages'. (p. 60)
    Explain this statement.
12. What was Charlemagne's favourite book?
13. 'Charlemagne could give the Church peace'. (p. 61)
    What could the Pope of Rome give to the Emperor of the Romans?
14. What were 'the two cities'?
15. For what reason did the Emperor make an alliance with the Khazars?

16. (a) To what post did the Emperor appoint Constantine?
(b) What was Constantine's life work, and who shared that work with him?
(c) What discovery did Constantine make in the Crimea?
(d) Why did the Emperor not send a bishop to Moravia?
(e) In what ways did Constantine and Methodius help to bring together the Church of the East and the Church of the West?
17. (a) By what other name is Constantine sometimes known, and why?
(b) When did he die and at what age?
18. (a) Who was Rastislav, and what was his hope for his people?
(b) Where and when was his hope fulfilled?
19. (a) On what powers did Vladimir depend at the time when he became ruler of Kiev?
(b) What was his attitude to religion, and which religion did he choose for his people?
(c) Why do Russians sometimes call him 'equal to the Apostles'?

DISCUSSION AND RESEARCH

20. 'Some Christians wished that the work of the Church had been kept clear of politics'. (pp. 57, 58)
Do you think it is right for the Church to keep clear of politics? Do you think it is possible? Give reasons for your answers.
21. 'Charles Martel shared the Franks' ideas that in expanding their rule eastwards they were bringing civilization and peace.' (p. 58)
What nations or national leaders have had similar ideas in more modern times?
How far, if at all, do you think that their ideas—and those of the Franks—were justified?
22. Do you know of any book or books which have influenced religious and political leaders of modern times, as Augustine's *City of God* influenced the Pope and the Emperor of the Romans? If so, what sort of influence was it, and what have been the results?
23. Read again the stories about the reactions of Vladimir's envoys and of the Japanese boy to the experience of worship in the Church of the East. (p. 70)
Do you think that a stranger would react in that way to the experience of worship in your own Church? Give reasons for your answer. In what other circumstances than worship in church might a stranger feel: '. . . we did not know whether we were in heaven or on earth . . .'? (p. 70)
24. Vladimir sent envoys to examine the religions of neighbouring countries and advise him which one he and the people he ruled should follow (see p. 68). Give examples, if you can, of any present-day rulers who have chosen an 'official' religion for their people to follow. What was the people's reaction?

CHAPTER 6

Muslims, Mongols, Crusades, and Friars

MUSLIMS ON THE MOVE

About the year 1000, horsemen from the high lands of Central Asia (see map 2, p. 17) were moving westward, much as the Huns had done 500 years before (Vol. 1, p. 118). They were a family called Seljuk, and the family had grown to become a clan, and the clan a tribe, and the tribe a people. They came from Turkistan, and are therefore called the Seljuk Turks. By 1055 they occupied the whole region which had once been Persia. These Turks had already become Muslim. They were nomad warriors, and were more like Persia's first Muslim invaders than the cultured Arabs who now enjoyed a soft and settled life in Bagdad. The Seljuk Turks did not displace the *Khalif* (i.e. 'Successor' of Muhammad) as this state's religious head, but their leader took the title *Sultan* (i.e. 'Ruler'), and that is what he was.

From Bagdad the Sultan soon extended his rule to include Syria and Palestine, countries which till then had been under the rival Khalifate of Egypt. The next powerful country to the westward was the Eastern Roman Empire, sometimes called the Byzantine Empire (Byzantium was the name of Constantinople before the time of the Emperor Constantine). In 1071 the Seljuk Turks met the Emperor's army at Manzikert in Armenia. They destroyed the army, captured the Emperor, and advanced across Asia Minor. The Christian capital itself lay just across the narrow waters. The people of that part of the Eastern Roman Empire which remained could do nothing but call fellow-Christians of the west to their aid.

In 1095 at Clermont in France Pope Urban II proclaimed the first Crusade (i.e. campaign under the Cross):

'Refrain your hands from killing your brothers.
As soldiers of the Faith, turn your hands against foreign nations, and under Jesus Christ your leader, as a Christian army, an army invincible, better than the Israelites of old, you shall do battle for your Jerusalem, and attack and expel the Turks there, who are worse than the Jebusites.' (Kidd, *Documents* III, pp. 136–138)

TWO PROBLEMS

We must notice what the Pope was trying to do. He was solving *two*

73

problems at once, and was doing it by suggesting *more positive* action. The first problem was the turbulence of feudal society; the second was the Emperor's appeal for help.

1. THE TURBULENCE OF FEUDAL SOCIETY

The social order which had been taking shape since the fall of the Western Roman Empire before the barbarian invasions, was that which is called Feudalism. 'Feu' is the same word as 'fee', meaning 'payment for services given'. Barbarian chieftains had rewarded their followers with gifts of land, and as the new population settled, use of the land continued to be regarded as payment for military service by men to their lord (whether head of a whole kingdom, or a local land-owner within a kingdom). The men, besides getting use of the land, were safer under the lord's protection.

We call feudalism a social *order*, but in some ways it encouraged *dis*order. Since each lord had an army which he could call if a quarrel arose, quarrels did constantly arise.

The Church in this period tried to reduce war-making by what was called 'the Truce (i.e. Peace) of God'. This was a rule forbidding fighting from Saturday night to Monday morning. It may seem strange to us—treating war-makers in the same way as shopkeepers, with a rule for Sunday closing. But the power of the Church was great, and the rule was so successful that Thursday, Friday, and Saturday were added later as non-fighting days. In his proclamation at Clermont Pope Urban was attempting something more positive. He was saying, 'Instead of Christian fighting Christian, join together to face the real enemy, the danger in the east.'

2. THE EMPEROR'S APPEAL FOR HELP

Here again the Pope's proclamation was more positive. The Emperor wanted defence against the Seljuk Turks' attack. The Pope proclaimed an aggressive campaign to regain the Holy Land for Christendom. This caught men's imagination, and there resounded throughout Europe the answering cry, 'Deus vult!' (Latin for 'God wills it'). The Pope acted as the Head of Christendom, and his proclamation did actually place him at the head of Europe. The Crusades were the first attempt of the new peoples of Europe to act together. But the Crusades did not wait for kings and governments to organize and act— they began immediately as a people's movement, the first in European history.

Crowds gathered in churches, in market squares, at the cross-roads, to listen to wandering preachers who passed on the call. It was like a recruiting campaign, except that there was no army to join—nothing ready at all, no armaments, or food, or transport. In parts of Europe

6.1 In 1095 at Clermont in France Pope Urban II proclaimed the first Crusade to recapture the Holy Land from the Turks. A wood engraving of 1522 shows the Pope with knights and bishops in council.

6.2 'The crusades opened the way eastward' (p. 77). Evidence of this is seen in the ruins of castles like this one, which the crusaders built in what are now Jordan, the Lebanon and Syria, as well as Palestine itself.

men sold their farms, put the family and a few household goods into an ox-waggon, and joined the procession straggling eastward. They knew nothing of foreign lands, distance, or danger. In this first tragic 'People's Crusade' of 1096 some went for the adventure, some for hope of gain, and some because they knew, however vaguely, that there was an enemy in the east and that western Christians could, and would, do something about it. But few of them can have got as far as Palestine, and none ever got home again.

THE CRUSADES: GAIN AND LOSS

In 1096, after the tragedy of the People's Crusades, regular armies, such as the Emperor had hoped for, set out from France and Italy, wintered at Constantinople, and in 1097 fought their way across Asia Minor, restoring it to the Eastern Roman Empire. They captured Antioch, and in 1099 besieged and took Jerusalem. In Syria and Palestine they set up a group of four states, based upon Edessa, Antioch, Tripoli, and Jerusalem (map 5, p. 88). This was a surprising series of victories within three years. No later Crusade achieved anything like so much.

In reading history we have to make judgements upon history. Today most people agree that the Crusades were a tragic blunder. Their military failure is shown by the fact that between 1096 and 1291 there had to be eight Crusades. The first ended in victory. The other seven were attempts to stop the fruits of victory from being snatched away. Yet they were snatched away, and by 1291, with the fall of Acre, the last fortress on the coast of Palestine, nothing was left of all that the Crusades had won. Two centuries of intermittent fighting had shown that peoples of the west could take Palestine but could not hold it.

The original call for help had been to defend the Eastern Roman Empire from the Seljuk Turks. Men of the Fourth Crusade, setting out to attack Egypt, had turned instead against the Eastern Roman Empire, pillaged Constantinople, and permanently weakened it. That was why in 1453 the Christian capital was easily captured by another wave of invading Turks, the Ottomans. The memory of the Fourth Crusade has deepened the tragic division between Greek and Latin Christians. And memories of two centuries of war caused most Muslims and Christians to go on thinking of the enmity between them, rather than of those beliefs which both religions share.

On the side of gain, two things must be said:

1. The Crusades were the first attempt of the new peoples of the west to act together and to act in a Christian cause. This was a gain, even if the attempt ended in failure, and the cause turned out to be not so Christian after all.

2. And the Crusades opened the way eastward, to the surviving higher civilization of the Eastern Roman Empire and to the wider world beyond. Later in this chapter we shall follow travellers and missionaries, even to the furthest end of Asia.

THE STORY OF PRESTER JOHN

The first Crusade ended in triumph in 1099. Syria and Palestine were held under the Christian rule of four Latin states (p. 76 and map 5, p. 88). But the first Crusaders grew old, and sailed for home or died. The scattered forces of Islam recovered and regrouped, and they struck the counter-blow in 1144. The result was the fall of Edessa, most important of the four Crusader states. People began to ask themselves: 'Are the Crusades doomed to end in defeat?'

At this point we first hear of Prester John. Evidently some one was trying to give a hopeful answer to that question. The story of Prester John (i.e. John 'the Priest') told of a mighty kingdom to the east, beyond the dreaded Muslims, and of a Christian king—so zealous a Christian that he was in priest's orders—whose armies would take them in the rear. Twenty years later a letter was passed round the courts of Europe which was supposed to have come from Prester John:

'We have planned to visit the sepulchre of our Lord at the head of a great army, to combat and humble the enemies of the cross of Christ . . . Our territory stretches from India, where lies the body of St Thomas the Apostle, across the deserts to the place where the sun is born, and back by the ruins of Babylon not far from the Tower of Babel—on one side the length of a four months' journey, on the other side no one can know how great it is.'

These heartening stories continued through a century and a half. Popes, emperors, and kings wrote to Prester John, and sent ambassadors to find him. Was there any truth in the story at all?

THE TRUTH: CHRISTIANS AMONG THE MONGOLS

We have already followed the earlier outreaching of the Church of the East to the capital of China in 635, and have noted its disappearance from China about the year 900 (pp. 41 and 51). The truth behind the Prester John legend was that Christianity had not disappeared from Central Asia. Soon after the year 1000 we find it spreading eastward again, this time by a more northerly route.

We hear, for example, a report to the *Catholicos* (i.e. Patriarch) of the East from the Archbishop of Merv, about the king of a nomad people called the Keraits:

'The Crusades: gain and loss: two centuries of intermittent fighting had shown that the people of the west could take Palestine but.could not hold it.' (p. 76)

Scenes from the fourteenth-century French Chronicles of St Denis show crusading knights:

6.3   Besieging the coastal fortress of Damietta; and

6.4   Being lured to their deaths by the treachery of the Saracens.

'He called to him Christian merchants who were in his country and asked them about the Faith . . . He received from them a Gospel which he worships daily. And now he has sent a messenger to ask me to go to him or send a priest to baptize him.'

We know that there were Christians among the Uighars and Naimans of West Mongolia, the Merkites south of Lake Baikal, and by 1100 even among Tartars and Onguts of East Mongolia (see map 5, p. 88).

The thirteenth century was a time of Mongol power—the Mongols being another group of nomad tribesmen east of the Keraits. The Mongols' empire was soon to become *in fact* greater than Prester John's *in fancy*. Nothing was able to withstand the whirlwind assault of these horsemen. The Keraits were their nearest neighbours, and were first overrun and absorbed in 1202. By 1238 they had swept across Asia and were entering Europe. In 1241 they were approaching Vienna. Rome itself trembled. But the advance suddenly stopped. Europe breathed again, and no one knew why. The fact was that, half-way across the world in Karakorum, the Great Khan (king) of all the Mongols, Ogotai, was dead, and Batu his nephew, who led this westward attack, had to return to Mongolia to consult about his successor.

People in the west continued to believe in the Prester John romance because it comforted them. They connected it vaguely with one or other of the Khans of the Mongol confederacy, and occasionally found fresh evidence of Christians in the east. Both reasons—fear of Mongol invaders, and hope of discovering a Christian power among them—led western Christendom to send ambassadors. The first was an Italian Franciscan, John of Pian di Carpine who went in 1245. The last, again an Italian Franciscan, was John of Marignolli, who arrived back from China in 1353. In between, there were two Dominicans. All confirmed the 'Prester John' story in this respect: while the advancing wave of Mongols had, from 1202 onwards, flowed over the Christian kingdoms of the Keraits, these, and other peoples who were Christian or largely Christian, had remained to influence their conquerors. The Mongol conquest was at first a wave of destruction, but the flood eventually carried Christians to positions that were higher than Christians had ever held in eastern lands before.

KUBLAI KHAN AND THE POPE

Genghis Khan, founder of the Mongol Empire, had a younger son, who married a Kerait princess. Chinese records say that she was buried in a *shih-tzu-ssu* (figure ten monastery). Figure ten in Chinese is $+$, so this can be translated 'monastery of the cross'. Syriac ecclesiastical records say, 'She was a true believer, like Helena' (mother of the

Emperor Constantine). Her three sons show signs of remembering their Christian parentage. Mangu had a Christian wife. He became Great Khan in 1251, i.e. head of the whole Mongol confederacy stretching right across Asia and direct ruler of Mongolia from his capital, Karakorum. Hulagu became first Mongol ruler (Ilkhan) of Persia. He too married a Christian princess, daughter of the Eastern Roman Emperor himself. She made him spare the lives of Christians when he stormed Bagdad. Kublai was governor of China under his brother Mangu, and then in 1259 succeeded him as Great Khan.

Kublai moved the capital to Peking, which was called Khanbalik, city of the Khan. His Empire was the widest that the world had ever known, stretching from the China Sea westward to the river Danube, and from the Ural mountains south to the Himalayas. And this was the Great Khan who gave to the Christian Church its greatest chance. News of it was brought to the Pope by two merchants of Venice who returned from Kublai's capital in 1269, Nicolo and Maffeo Polo. These were Kublai's words to his father and uncle, as Marco Polo, Nicolo's son, later reported them:

'How can you expect me to become a Christian? You see that Christians in these parts are so ignorant that they do nothing and have no power ... But you shall go to your High Priest (Pope) and shall pray him to send me a hundred men skilled in your religion . . . And so I shall be baptized, and then all my barons and great men, and then their subjects, and so there will be more Christians here than there are in your parts.'

The Mongols in their nomad life had been simple spirit worshippers. Now they were rulers of a vast empire.

Kublai knew what civilization he intended to follow: that of China, a choice which he made when he moved his capital to Peking. But the Mongols were wavering in their choice of a religion. There were there possibilities: they knew Islam in the west of their territories, Buddhism in the east, and Christianity scattered over the whole. By the year 1300 the choice had gone against Christianity: in the west to Islam, in the east to Buddhism. But, for at least thirty years before, there was a chance that it might be Christianity for them all.

In reply to Kublai's request, Pope Gregory X sent, to accompany the Polos, not a hundred missionaries, but two Dominican Friars. The stories of his father and uncle had stirred the heart of Marco, then seventeen and a half years old. He must go with them on their second journey, It was twenty-four years before he saw Venice again, most of those years having been spent in positions of high influence under the Great Khan. There was no religious call about this—just love of adventure. Of the two Dominicans, Marco says that they endured until they met warfare in Armenia:

'And when the Brothers Preachers saw this they had great fear to go farther. Then they said they will not go at all.'

So passed the greatest missionary opportunity in the history of the Church.

TWO MONKS FROM CHINA: SAUMA AND MARK

A few years later, two monks were making the same dreadful journey across Asia, but this time they were monks from China travelling westwards. Their names were Sauma and Mark, and they were Ongut by race, from a small monastery near Peking. They had set out on pilgrimage to the Holy Land. The Muslim Turks closed the way, but they were presented to their *Catholicos* (Patriarch) at the city of Maragha (see map 5, p. 88), and (as they said afterwards) 'felt as if they had seen the Lord Himself'.

The Catholicos ordained Mark as bishop, and sent him back to be Metropolitan of China. But everything seemed to go wrong. The way back to China was closed by war. They returned to the Catholicos but found him dead. The bishops were gathering to elect his successor, so, as bishop, Mark went too. The others felt Mark's presence to be providential. Here was a bishop from Khanbalik, capital of all the Mongols, who knew the Mongol language and Mongol ways. They elected him. So in 1281 a monk from Peking became Catholicos of the East—ruler of the Church which stretched from Mesopotamia to the China Sea.

The Mongol Khan who ruled what had been Persia was Kublai's nephew. He too had a Christian mother, the daughter of the Eastern Roman Emperor (p. 80). He chose the other monk from China, Sauma, to go as his ambassador to the courts of the west, with promises of Mongol alliance if the Christian nations would raise one more Crusade —promising indeed to make the Prester John dream come true. His travel diary still exists. To read it is to see the medieval west through oriental eyes.

Sauma went first to Constantinople, and marvelled, as we have done (in chapter 1), at the church of the Holy Wisdom with 'a dome incredibly high'. From there he sailed to Rome, where he surprised the cardinals (the Pope's chief officials) by saying:

'Many Mongols are Christians. Kings and Queens have been baptized. No one came to us from the Pope. The Apostle Thomas taught our ancestors, and we hold that which they handed down.'

6.5 and 6.6   News of the Mongol Empire was brought to the Pope by two merchants of Venice, Nicolo and Maffeo Polo, who returned from Kublai Khan's capital in 1269.

Illustrations in the French *Book of Martyrs*, Nicolo's son Marco Polo's account of their travels, show the two brothers carrying messages between Pope Gregory X and the Great Khan.

Then Sauma rode through France, and at Paris was guest of King Philip the Fair, and saw Europe's first university. Sauma says that it had 30,000 students, but students were unruly then (as they often still can be) and so seemed more numerous than they really were. The Sauma journeyed for twenty days, and at Bordeaux was presented to some one whom he calls 'the king of Alanguitar'. He means *Angleterre*, which is French for England. The king was Edward I, who had a position in the French feudal system as Duke of Aquitaine, this part of France. The king asked him to celebrate the Eucharist, and the monk from China used his Syriac liturgy. As they later said at Rome, 'The language is different, but the rite is one.' And there the king of England knelt to receive the sacrament from the hands of a monk from China. This is one of those flashes on the screen of history, where one sees things as God meant them to be.

NEW MONASTIC ORDERS—
MILITARY, AND THE FRIARS

In every period when new life stirs within the Church, that life seems to express itself in the forming of new monastic Orders. It was so in the period of the Crusades. The Orders most obviously connected were the military ones, of soldier-monks. As monks they took vows of poverty, chastity, and obedience. As soldiers they promised military service. The two most famous were (1) the Knights Templar (i.e. of the Temple), so called because their base in Jerusalem was near the site of the Temple; and (2) the Knights of St John, whose purpose was to care for sick and wounded Crusaders, and whose base was in a hospital near the Church of St John Baptist in Jerusalem.

The Orders of 'Friars' (i.e. Brothers) began in this period also. They differed from monks in not being confined to a monastery but going about as preachers and teachers among the people. The two most famous Orders of Friars are the Franciscans, founded by St Francis in 1209, also called the Order of Brothers Minor (Lesser); and the Dominicans, founded by St Dominic in 1216, also called the Order of Brothers Preachers. The Dominicans were indirectly connected with the Crusades because they were often, as preachers, used by the Pope to encourage people to give or to go. Also, all the envoys sent to the lands of the Mongols by the Pope, as we saw (pp. 79, 80), were either Franciscans or Dominicans, and so were outstanding missionaries of the period. We shall deal with Dominic and his Order in more detail when we return to the subject of the coming of the Friars as one of the medieval movements for reform (pp. 149–150). The Franciscans were directly connected with the Crusades from their very origin—

from Francis himself. So we must give special attention to him here as well as in the later section.

ST FRANCIS

The man whom we call St Francis was born in Assisi in Italy (map 3B, p. 32) in 1181. The main street of Assisi today looks not very different from the street which he knew. Many buildings are as old as that. One building, still there, is a pre-Christian temple, built under the Romans *centuries* before the time of St Francis. Much of Italy, in areas where there is no modern industry, has remained unchanged for hundreds of years.

The saint was not christened 'Francis'. His father, a cloth merchant, had had to go to France, and, coming back, greeted the new baby as 'little Frenchman', or in Italian, 'Francesco' (pronounced Fran-chess-co). So he was the first man to take that for a name. He was to be the first man to do many things.

Francis's father often told the boy of knights riding to adventure on the roads of France. As the boy grew up he allowed him enough money to have a horse to ride, and to share the fun—and sometimes adventure too—with young nobles of the district. Francis was taken prisoner in 1202 in a local war. Gay, generous, a leader among men, he dreamed of a great future, and perhaps a knightly one.

Then, after a serious illness, he began to change. On a pilgrimage to Rome, he changed clothes with a beggar, to see what a day in the life of the poor was like. He began helping those with leprosy, a disease which everybody then, and he himself, dreaded. In 1208 he heard the words of Matthew 10.7–19 read in church, and felt that they were spoken to himself, as a call to preach, tend the sick and lepers, have no money, be ready to suffer, and, in it all, not to be anxious.

Francis's father thought him mad, and disowned him, but he began to have a few followers. In 1209 he and eleven companions went to Rome. The Pope feared that their rule of absolute poverty might be too strict, but recognized them as an Order. They chose the humble name 'the Penitents of Assisi', later changed to Brothers Minor (Lesser Brothers).

In 1212 a girl of noble family, Clare, was admitted, and this was the beginning of the Second Franciscan Order, for Women, generally called the Poor Clares. In 1221 there began the Third Order, for men and women who did not leave ordinary life but accepted St Francis's ideals, lived simply and faithfully, and were generous in gifts to the Church and service of the needy. Love of nature and of song, and an underlying gaiety of spirit, marked all the years of Francis's life. He died on 3 October 1226, in the church in which he had heard his call.

Francis had shared with the youth of his time ideals about being a knight. But, after his call, these ideals had developed further. He went out to protect the weak and relieve the oppressed, but he no longer went with a strong horse and sharp sword. He did it by sharing the life of beggars and taking care of lepers. Francis went on to 'take the cross'—words used of a knight when he joined a Crusade. In 1219, during the Fifth Crusade, he reached Egypt, but his adventure was to pass unarmed through the ranks of Muslim soldiers, and stand as a missionary of Christ before the Sultan of Egypt. His way was to win the Holy Land not by fighting the Muslims but by converting them.

The Pope had proclaimed the First Crusade to direct the turbulence of feudal society towards a Christian end. Francis went to Egypt expecting martyrdom, and ready for it. For Francis, not just the end, but the *means* also were Christian.

MISSIONS OF THE FRIARS

In 1221 both of the great Orders of Friars committed themselves to missionary work. Francis added this to the Rule of his Order:

'Whoever of the Brothers, inspired by God, shall desire to go among Muslims or other unbelievers, let them go . . . And let all the Brothers, wherever they may be, remember they have given themselves and surrendered their bodies to our Lord Jesus Christ, for love of whom they ought to expose themselves to their enemies both visible and invisible.'

The Dominican Order, meeting at Bologna, accepted the words of Mark 16.15, 'Go into all the world', as a command to themselves. Dominicans were soon at work in eastern Europe and what is now south Russia, and Friars of both Orders entered the Middle East.

In 1289 John of Montecorvino, an Italian Franciscan, was sent east by the Pope, and John mentions Nicholas, a Dominican, as 'companion of my journey'. John had been a missionary in Persia, and was encouraged by the pro-Christian Ilkhan Arghun (see p. 80) to go to the capital of all the Mongols. The Pope gave his blessing, and wrote letters to the Great Khan and to the Catholicos of the East. John went from Persia by sea to 'the country of India and the Church of St Thomas' (i.e. Mylapore), where his Dominican colleague died, so he went on alone. His arrival was twenty-five years after Kublai Khan's appeal for 100 missionaries, and Kublai died that same year 1294. The opportunity had passed.

John's report to the Pope in 1305 tells of winning King George of the Onguts, who were 'Nestorians', in what is now Shensi Province, 'to the true Catholic Faith'. This naturally set the Church of the East against him. They put out rumours that he was a spy, and he was arrested several times in his first five years there. Nevertheless his letter claims 6,000 converts in Khanbalik, and 'it might have been 30,000 but for the slanders'. His letters describe his method of work.

'I have built a church in the city . . . and brought 40 boys between the ages of seven and eleven, untrained in religion, and have baptized them and taught them Latin, and our Liturgy. I have written for them thirty Psalters with Hymnaries and two Breviaries. Eleven of them now know our Office and maintain the choir services whether I am there or not . . . And the Lord Emperor is greatly delighted with their chanting. I strike the bells at all the Hours (the eight times for services, see p. 144) and perform the divine Office with my congregation of babes and sucklings. But we sing by heart because we have no service-book with notes.'

It may sound inappropriate to teach Latin, and have daily services exactly as in the west, but John believed that Christian worship was Christian witness.

John's method was not everywhere so western. Among the Onguts he celebrated the Eucharist in a Mongol language. He said he had translated the New Testament and Psalter, and had 'preached openly and in public'. He made pictures of Old and New Testament subjects 'for teaching those who cannot read'.

In 1307 the Pope consecrated seven Franciscans as bishops, with instructions to consecrate John as their archbishop, and then serve under him. Only three survived the dreadful journey. Some other churches were opened, in Khanbalik, in Ch'uan-chou the sea-port, and in Yang-chou on the Grand Canal, but nothing like a Province resulted, though that had obviously been the Pope's hope, in making so many bishops.

In 1321 four Franciscans, recruits for this mission, changed ships at Thana, the port for what is now Bombay. While they waited for a junk going to China, Syrian Christians there gave them shelter. But they were discovered and killed, the first known Christian martyrs in India—Thomas, James, Peter, and Demetrius.

The tragedy of this first mission from the Church of the West to East Asia was that it arrived too late for the mass-movement which Kublai had foretold, and it remained too small—instead of a hundred missionaries a mere handful. It had two other weaknesses: it failed to co-operate with the Church of the East, and it failed to reach the people of the land.

1. CO-OPERATION

When Sauma was in Rome (p. 81), he was invited to celebrate the

Eucharist, using his Syrian Liturgy, before the Pope. And the next Sunday he was the first communicant at the Pope's own celebration. He left with presents from the Pope for his own Catholicos. No difficulty was raised about difference of tradition.

The mission from the west, even where it was represented only by one solitary priest, failed to co-operate with fellow-Christians already present in strength—indeed from the outset the missionaries tried to compete and supplant, instead of coming as a mission of help (p. 74). If intercommunion was practical in Rome, co-operation should have been possible in Peking.

2. REACHING THE PEOPLE OF THE LAND

Christians of whom we hear in the letters of the missionaries are all of non-Chinese race—officials, soldiers, merchants, or immigrant tribes who have entered China under the Mongol dynasty. One exception is in a letter from Bishop Peregrine of Ch'uan-chou, the seaport, written in 1318. It mentions crowds in the street, and it must surely mean Chinese, whose language the Friars did not know.

'We have good hope when we see the people intent on hearing, and running to where we are preaching. We truly believe that if we had their tongues, wonderful works of God would be seen. The harvest truly is great but the labourers are few, and with no sickle. For we are but a few Friars, and very old, and unable to learn the language. May God forgive those who hinder Friars from coming.'

In 1368 the Mongol dynasty came to an end. Keraits and Uighars, Naimans and Merkites, Tartars and Onguts, moved out of China. And, with them Christianity for the second time disappeared from the East Asian scene. If a *Chinese* Church had been founded, it would have remained.

MISSIONARY STATESMAN AND MARTYR, RAMON LULL, 1315

Ramon Lull was a Spaniard, born in Majorca in 1235, soon after the island was freed from Muslim rule. In 1263, a dissolute young courtier, he was composing a love-song, and, gazing into space, felt that some one was there gazing back at him. He looked again, and this is what he said:

'I saw our Lord Jesus Christ hanging on the cross in great agony and sorrow'.

The vision came again, and again. This is his confession:

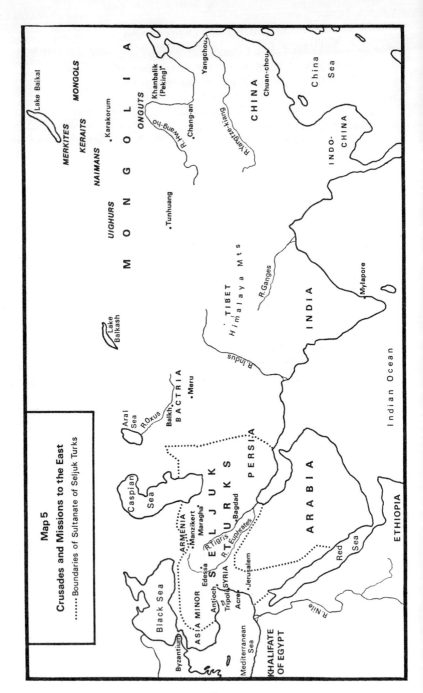

Map 5

Crusades and Missions to the East

...... Boundaries of Sultanate of Seljuk Turks

Lake Baikal

MERKITES

KERAITS   *MONGOLS*

NAIMANS

• Karakorum

UIGHURS   ONGUTS   Khanbalik
                                (Peking)*

M   O   N   G   O   L   I   A   • Chang-an   Yangchou•

R.Hwang-ho

• Tunhuang   CHINA   Chuan-chou•

Lake
Balkash   China
                                                    Sea

TIBET   INDO-
        Himalaya Mts   CHINA

Aral
Sea   R.Ganges

R.Oxus   Balkh•
          BACTRIA   I   N   D   I   A

          •Meru

Caspian   R.Indus   •Mylapore
Sea

                    P E R S I A

ARMENIA   Indian Ocean
  •Manzikert
  Maragha•
S E L J U K   •Bagdad
  R.Tigris R.Euphrates

ASIA MINOR   T   U   R   K   S   A R A B I A

Antioch• SYRIA
Edessa•
Tripoli•   •Jerusalem   Red
Acre•   Sea   ETHIOPIA

Byzantium•

Black Sea

Mediterranean
Sea

KHALIFATE
OF EGYPT

R.Nile

88

'In the best time of my youth, O Lord, I gave myself wholly to sin. Now I will give to Thee both myself and all that is mine.'

As a courtier, Lull naturally thought of Christ's service as a Crusade, but he joined the Third Order of Franciscans because he saw (as Francis had done, p. 85), that the real Crusade was to try to win Muslims for Christ. 'If they were converted,' he wrote, 'it would be easy to convert the rest of the world.'

Lull's only training had been for court life, so, at the age of thirty, he had to start again as a schoolboy. In spite of his late start, he became a famous theologian, and, more important, the greatest missionary statesman since Pope Gregory the Great (p. 24). He believed that missionary work required three means: language, learning, and life.

1. LANGUAGE

Ramon Lull advised the Pope to have the best linguists and preachers selected, and then put aside one tenth of the whole income of the Church to support colleges for training them. He went around the universities of Europe, and influenced Rome, Bologna, Paris, Oxford, and Salamanca to advance the studies of Hebrew, Arabic, Syriac, and Greek. He himself became a distinguished Arabic and Islamics scholar.

2. LEARNING

Lull wrote many books, the biggest being a reasoned argument which, he believed, would *compel* non-Christians to accept the Faith. This is his verse about it:

'A system I have found that's new
By which comes knowledge of the true,
And falsehood's followers grow few,
Mongol, Muhammadan, and Jew.'

Lull may have overstated the importance of reason. But this overstatement provided a necessary balance to the attitude of St Francis, who gave no place to learning. He was afraid that it might spoil the simplicity of the Gospel for his Friars. A missionary needs the exhortation of 1 Peter 3.15, which joins the learning of Lull to the gentleness of Francis. Lull believed in the possibility of dialogue with Muslim leaders. He developed relationships of mutual respect with some of them, and was ready to answer such a challenge as was given by one:

'If you hold that the law of Christ is true, and that of Muhammad false, you must prove it by reason.'

Notice that Lull in the rhyme already quoted recognized the Mongols, and the opportunity of winning them. He wrote:

'Their own religion is primitive, and they allow missionaries free entry. But if the Mongols set up a new religion, as Muhammad did, all Christendom would be in peril.'

3. LIFE

Lull's own three missions to Muslims in North Africa illustrate his methods. The first was to Tunis in 1291, when his fluent language drew the crowd, but his learned dialogue ended in arrest and banishment. The second was at Bugia in Algiers in 1307, where instead of learned debate, the result was prison, with a mob outside the grating. He crossed to both places again in 1315, when his dialogues at Tunis caused less offence because of respect for his age—he was eighty. But at Bugia the crowd was hostile. Lull himself had written:

'Missionaries will convert the world by preaching, but also through the shedding of tears and blood, and with great labour, and through a bitter death.'

Outside the city gate, in a hail of stones, Ramon Lull followed St Stephen the first martyr.

STUDY SUGGESTIONS

WORD STUDY

1. (a) What is the origin of the word 'feudal'?
   (b) Describe in your own words, with examples, how the feudal system worked.
2. Why was the Eastern Roman Empire sometimes called the Byzantine empire?

REVIEW OF CONTENT

3. (a) Who were the Muslim horsemen who moved westward from Central Asia about the year 1000, and which countries did they invade?
   (b) What was the name of their ruler?
4. (a) In what year was the Eastern Roman Emperor defeated and captured by Muslims, and where?
   (b) What did the people of the Empire then do?
5. In 1095 Pope Urban II proclaimed the first crusade. What two problems was this to solve?
6. Who or what were the following?
   (a) Crusades (b) Prester John (c) Keraits (d) *Catholicos*
7. What was the 'Truce of God'?
8. (a) What is meant by the statement (pp. 73, 74). that in his proclama-

tion of a crusade, Pope Urban was 'attempting something more positive'?

(b) What is meant by the statement (p. 74) that the Pope 'acted as the head of Christendom'?

9. What was the 'People's Crusade' in 1095, and why was it a tragedy?

10. (a) Over roughly what period did the Crusades take place?
(b) Which, if any, of the Crusades were successful?

11. (a) What were two important *bad* results of the Crusades?
(b) What were two important *good* results of the Crusades?

12. (a) Name five tribes of Mongolia among whom there were Christians in the eleventh and twelfth centuries AD.
(b) Name two Mongol Khans who had Christian wives.

13. (a) Which was the Great Khan who 'gave the Christian Church its greatest chance'?
(b) Where was his capital?

14. What religion did the Mongols eventually choose for their empire?

15. Compare Pope Gregory X's action in sending a mission to Mongolia (p. 80) with the action of Pope Gregory I in sending a mission to England. What were the results in each case?

16. Who were the Friars, and what was the chief difference between them and most other monastic orders?

17. (a) What sort of life did Francis of Assisi live before he became a monk, and what made him leave that life?
(b) In what way did the Pope think that the rule followed by Francis and his companions might be too strict?
(c) What part did Francis take in the Crusades, and when?

18. 'In 1221 both great Orders of Friars committed themselves to missionary work' (p. 85). How did each do this?

19. 'The Pope directed the turbulence of feudal society towards a Christian *end*' (p. 85), i.e. that of winning back the Holy Land for Christendom.
In what ways did Francis and others try to achieve that end by Christian *means*?

20. (a) Who was John of Montecorvino?
(b) To what countries was he sent as missionary?
(c) Describe some of his missionary methods and some of the difficulties he faced?

21. (a) Name the first four known Christian martyrs in India. When they were killed and how?
(b) What were the chief weaknesses of the Church's first mission to east Asia?

22. (a) In what ways was Ramon Lull's early life like that of Francis of Assisi?
(b) What else did he share with Francis?

(c) In what ways did his missionary attitude 'balance' that of Francis?

(d) What did he share with Stephen (see Acts 7.54–60)?

DISCUSSION AND RESEARCH

23. (a) What were the three chief 'means' required for missionary work, according to Ramon Lull, and how did he acquire and use them?

(b) To what extent have these same means been used by missionaries in your own country?

24. (a) Describe the adventures of the two monks from China, Sauma and Mark, when they travelled to the west.

(b) Explain the phrase 'one sees things as God meant them to be' (p. 83). What things, if any, do we see today, which are 'as God meant them to be'?

(c) Where do you think that travellers from East Asia to the west today would find 'things as God meant them to be'?

25. (a) Name the two most famous military monastic orders.

(b) What would you reply to someone who said: 'Military monastic orders are wrong. They contradict the teaching of Jesus in Matthew 6.24. A man cannot be a monk *and* a soldier. He cannot fulfil his vow of obedience to God and at the same time obey the orders of his military commander.'?

26. Find out all you can about the life and work of St Francis, and about the work of the Third Order of Franciscans today.

27. (a) How did John of Montecorvino teach the Faith to those who could not read?

(b) What methods of teaching the Faith to those who cannot read can the Church use today, which John of Montecorvino could not use? Does your own Church use these methods? Could it use them more widely than it does?

28. Find out what missionary work, if any, has been done by Religious Orders of monks or nuns in your own country, either in the past or at the present time. Are any 'military' orders now at work there? If so, how 'military' is the work they do?

CHAPTER 7

Church Life in the Middle Ages

Western historians call the period covered by this book, AD 500–1500, 'the Middle Ages', because it lies between the decline of Roman civilization (about 500), and the *Renaissance* (French for Rebirth) or Revival of Learning (about 1500), which for Europe opens the modern age. To use this phrase 'Middle Ages' is to look at history from a western point of view. That is what we shall be doing in much of this chapter on Church Life in the Middle Ages. We shall consider:

1. The provision of churches as centres of local Christian life.
2. The Church in local life.
3. The training of the clergy.
4. The Church's use of local language.
5. Church buildings.
6. Three centuries of specially great church building.

Generally we shall start from the Church of the West, sometimes called Latin Christianity. But we shall remember to note differences among Christians of Greek tradition further east; and also among those called Syrian Christians, further east still, who at two different periods (see chapters 4 and 6) reached as far east as the Pacific Ocean.

Having mentioned the East, let us begin there.

THE PROVISION OF CHURCHES

The clue to what this first Church in China was like is found on the Monument of 781 (see p. 40). The Persian missionaries arrived in 635, translated some of their scriptures, and asked for the Emperor's approval.

The Emperor's answer was an edict of toleration and the announcement that he had given them a monastery in the capital for twenty-one monks. The place is not described fully, but we cannot be far wrong if we imagine a fairly large building in the style usual for temples in China. It was probably of brick, with a flight of wide granite steps up to the entrance, a porch with granite pillars at the top, with curved roofs and coloured roof-tiles flashing in the sun. The inscription describes such a building, but even more beautiful, as having 'roofs fair as pheasants in flight' (p. 49). Christian missionaries were not often so generously received, but at that time China was the wealthiest country in the world.

Turning to the far west, we see a less impressive picture, though Edwin, King of Northumbria in 627, was not merely tolerating the Christian religion but accepting it:

'The King built a wooden church while he was being prepared for baptism . . . in this city of York' (p. 31).

The Anglo-Saxons, like other German peoples (p. 96), had been used to building only with wood, and that is how York minster started. But some Christian gathering places began in an even simpler way.

An English nun, writing soon after the year 700, tells of a sick boy whose parents decided to offer him to God's service, if only God would spare his life:

'They promised this, not in church, but at the foot of the cross. It is the custom on the estates of good men, to have a cross, which is dedicated to our Lord and held in great reverence, set up in a prominent place for those who wish to come and pray.'

As yet, no church at all—instead a cross. This too would at first be wooden, later replaced with stone, and often carved. Hundreds of carved stone crosses are still standing in England, some of which were put up as early as the seventh century. A cross at the wayside must often have been the first sign that the Church had arrived. Such crosses are often called 'preaching crosses'. The most famous one in Britain is at Ruthwell, south of Dumfries. The cross is Anglo-Saxon, though the place is now part of Scotland. It is seventeen feet high. Carved on it are pictures of John the Baptist and the Lamb ('Behold the Lamb of God': John 1.36), the Annunciation, the Flight to Egypt, the healing of a blind man, Mary washing the feet of Jesus, the Crucifixion, and Christ in glory. Such a cross provided the preacher with visual aids, and if some in the congregation were wearied by the sermon, they could just look at the pictures of holy things and walk round to the other side of the cross for more.

The preacher was usually a monk from a neighbouring monastery. Some were priests as well as monks, or brought a priest with them to celebrate the Eucharist. Except in bigger places, most congregations had no priest of their own.

The nun we have quoted above wrote also about 'good men' who 'set up a cross' for villagers on their estates. More generous landowners gave some of their land for the support of a priest or priests.

A church which served a whole town, or from which clergy travelled over a wide countryside, usually had a number of priests who lived together under their bishop or a senior priest. They might be monks, but even if they were not, such a church was often called a 'minster' (from the word monastery), because its staff lived as a community

7.1 'A cross at the wayside must often have been the first sign thàt the Church had arrived . . . the most famous one in Britain is at Ruthwell' (p. 94). Now inside the Church there, it was put up by Eigfrith of Northumbria about 680.

Men and materials were brought from Rome to help in building some of the earliest stone churches in Britain.

7.2 The dedication stone of St Paul's, Jarrow, shows it was put up in 682.

7.3 Bede the historian knew it well, and an ancient chair still in the abbey is said to have been his.

under something like a monastic rule. The setting up of parishes, each with its parish priest, was a gradual process. In England the process was not complete till about 1200.

As we saw (p. 94) the Anglo-Saxons, like the other German peoples of northern Europe, built in wood. In many places the ruins of Roman buildings towered over their wooden huts, as if inviting them to use brick or stone instead. The Romans had left them not only examples of what to do, but the materials with which to do it. It is clear that this is how more substantial building often began. For example, in Chester they built a church on stone foundations which had been the Roman *forum* (central meeting place). There is still a church on the site today. Escomb, a Durham village, has a seventh-century church with a high chancel arch such as no Anglo-Saxons of that period could have built. They lifted it from a Roman ruin.

We must notice a difference as, from northern lands, we look farther south. Where barbarian invaders had not driven out the old population, but had settled among them, many things had been destroyed, but not everything. Newcomers among the population found themselves sharing the use of church-buildings from Roman times, some of them big and beautiful.

CHURCHES AS CENTRES OF
LOCAL CHRISTIAN LIFE

However simple it was, the church was usually the best building in the place. Often it was the only building worth looking at. The whole town or village was proud of its church, and the people filled it on Sundays and on many other days also. The church was the centre of the community, the place where people gathered for almost every sort of occasion.

The priest, like his church, was used for many purposes. He was better educated than his parishioners, and so took the lead in the affairs of the local community. He was a peace-maker in disputes, an adviser as well as chaplain of craft guilds, and director of the beginnings of drama. These dramas, held in church, and often making processions around it, were based on stories from the Gospels, the Parables, the Last Judgement, or Lives of the Saints. They were enlivened with extra characters, original dialogues, and many comic situations. In much of western Europe this was the beginning of drama for people who had never known the classical dramas of Greece and Rome. It was popular, in the local language, seldom written down, and all of it was Christian in origin.

The priest's chief task was, of course, the ministry of the Word and

Sacraments. He celebrated the Eucharist on Sunday and on feast days. Daily celebration came much later.

We should note that for the Church of the West at that time the language of Bible and liturgy was still Latin. As a result of the barbarian invasions most of the people spoke other languages, and Latin had become a 'literary' language used only by the learned few. We shall consider this important problem of language more fully below (p. 102). The priest was expected to teach his people the Lord's Prayer, the Creed, the Commandments, and the meaning of the Sacraments. They would get to know a Latin word or phrase here and there, but, more important, they came to know the order of the service and to share in some of the actions of the liturgy. They would kneel when they came into church, stand for the Gospel, and make the sign of the cross at the Creed. If there was a sermon, which happened on special occasions, e.g. when the bishop came, it would be in their own language, and so would the bidding prayer for the whole Church, the clergy, and the needs of all men. They knew when the bread and wine were consecrated, and knelt with the priest after the solemn words.

Frequent communions were expected only of clergy, monks, and nuns. The priest would instruct his people to come to him for confessions, especially during Lent, so as to be ready for the Easter Communion. He would sit in front of the altar, with a line of penitents waiting each in turn to kneel before him and speak words which only the two of them could hear. If a man or woman was slow in finding words, the priest might mention the seven deadly sins—pride, covetousness, lust, envy, gluttony, anger, sloth. Then the priest would advise, tell the penitent what he must do for his self-discipline, and then give him the comforting words, assuring him of Christ's forgiveness. We may remember that the Chinese inscription (p. 44) mentions the Sunday Eucharist, and connects it with 'cleansing the heart and regaining our purity'.

In a settled Christian community nearly all those brought for baptism were babies. They were immersed in the font and their foreheads were anointed with consecrated oil.

Children were confirmed at an early age, and confirmation was often a somewhat haphazard blessing given by the bishop as he was among the children, without any service in church at all.

Marriages also were brief. The vows were made, the ring put on, and blessing given, just within the church door.

The priest's duties included visiting the sick, with words of comfort and prayer for recovery, and, for those likely to die, the *viaticum*, Latin for 'provision for a journey'. This meant the last Communion, with the final blessing in the name of the Trinity, and an exhortation, 'Set out, Christian soul, from this world in peace.'

In studying the Early Church, we noted that men looked to the Church for help long before the state did anything for those in need (see Vol. 1, p. 28). This remained true in the Church of the Middle Ages. The priest would urge his people to remember the Seven Works of Mercy, which are giving food to the hungry, drink to the thirsty, shelter to the homeless, clothing to the naked, help for the sick, visits to prisoners, and burial to the dead. As we saw, four of these good works are mentioned in the eighth century Christian inscription in China (p. 49). In the west, people were encouraged to make bequests for such good works. Bishops were expected to use part of their income in providing for the poor, and from the ninth century onwards poor-houses were often established near the cathedral church.

With the growth of cities, of trade, and of wealth, many institutions were founded to care for the ill, the aged, and the needy. Such institutions were often marked as Christian by being dedicated to a saint and called by his name, e.g. one of the most famous hospitals is St Bartholomew's, London, founded in 1123. Through the centuries most works of mercy remained in the hands of the Church, or of institutions of Christian foundation. Almsgiving in the medieval Church prepared the way for modern systems of relief organized by the government, which began, as one might say, only yesterday.

TRAINING FOR THE CLERGY

In all this, so much depended upon the priests that we must ask how such men were chosen, and how they were trained for their task.

From the sixth century onwards education almost ceased in most lands of western Europe. Schools had been closed and teachers scattered because of the barbarian invasions. Education was carried on only in a few families who so valued learning that they preserved their books, and through the generations continued to pass on knowledge to their children. Among these privileged few were men who offered themselves for service in the Church, e.g. Pope Gregory the Great himself (see p. 24).

Training for Church service meant first of all learning to read, so it was better to begin in childhood. A devoted family would decide, often on the suggestion of priest or bishop, to dedicate a son to the Church. They would hand him over to the bishop to be brought up in his household, to live and learn and work with him. If the bishop lived with some of his clergy, as a religious community, one of their number would be put in charge of such boys. The bishop often taught them Latin, the language of all learning. He taught them also to say and to sing the service. And he taught them to count sufficiently well to reckon out the festivals of the Church year. This was not much of an education, but it was a beginning.

By the time of Bede in Northumbria (673–735), and Alcuin at the court of Charlemagne (735–804), such training had been extended to include something of what later became the accepted scheme for medieval education. This consisted of the *trivium* (Latin for 'three ways'), i.e. grammar, logic, rhetoric (i.e. style); and the *quadrivium* (Latin for 'four ways'), i.e. music, arithmetic, geometry, and astronomy.

The learners, while still very young, had their heads shaved to mark them as clergy, and were ordained as 'readers'. Sometimes boys were brought to an abbot instead of a bishop, and received their training among the monks. Some of the important people mentioned in previous chapters were educated in this way.

For example, Bede says of himself;

'I was given at the age of seven to be educated by the Abbot (at the monastery at Wearmouth) . . . I followed the monks' discipline, sang the daily service in church, and always held it good to learn, to teach, to write. At nineteen I was ordained deacon, and at thirty presbyter.'
(Bede, *Ecclesiastical History*, closing paragraph)

Bede used his monastery's splendid library to good purpose. We have called him 'the first English historian' (see p. 24). He was much more than that. He made himself one of the leading scholars of western Europe, and spent his life teaching others, till England had the best trained clergy anywhere outside Italy.

Another example is Willibrord, Apostle of the Netherlands (see p. 34). His biographer says of him;

'As soon as the child was weaned, his father gave him to the monks at Ripon.'

This reminds us of Hannah, as described in 1 Samuel 1.22–24, who brought her son Samuel, newly weaned, to the priest at Shiloh. In Willibrord's case it was his father; perhaps his mother had died. Bede records that Aidan had twelve boys training for the priesthood under him at Lindisfarne.

These examples from the Church of the west in the seventh century, are matched by the method which the Italian, John of Montecorvino, (see p. 86) used for training helpers in Peking seven hundred years later:

'Forty boys, between the ages of seven and eleven . . .
I have taught them Latin and our Liturgy . . .
I perform the divine office with my congregation of babes and sucklings.'

About the year 1050 came a burst of new life, expressing itself in the building of great churches which remain Europe's chief architectural splendour.

7.4 At Moissac in France the abbot read out the description of God's glory in Revelation 4.2–8, and asked the sculptor to carve it over the west door of the great church being built there.

7.5 To make churches safe from fire, architects developed the Roman art of stone-vaulting. Massive walls and pillars supporting the heavy roof made this Romanesque style look fortress-like. Durham Cathedral, built about 1100, is a good example.

This was the traditional training for clergy throughout the medieval Church of the West.

Professor Latourette, in his seven-volume *History of the Expansion of Christianity*, chose as title for the volume on the period AD 500–1500 'The Thousand Years of Uncertainty'. Here is an example of the uncertainty. With regard to training of the clergy in the time of Bede and Alcuin (i.e. 673–804), we have praised the high standard in England. Yet in 871 when Alfred became king, he gave this gloomy picture of the Church and its clergy:

> 'There were few south of the River Humber who could say what the Latin service books meant in English . . . and not many north of the Humber. South of the River Thames I cannot think of one . . . Thinking on these things, I thought also of what I had once seen, churches throughout all England full of treasures and of books, before all were looted and burned by the Northmen.' (The Introduction to Alfred's translation of Pope Gregory I's *Pastoral Care*)

By 'treasures' Alfred meant altar vessels of silver and gold, and shrines where relics were kept, ornamented with gold and precious stones. By 'books' he meant Bibles and service-books, many with ornamented lettering and illustrations in colours. But the greatest loss of all was represented by the priests themselves, who were now ignorant of the Latin in which Bible and prayer books were written. These were indeed the Dark Ages, and there were times when it was uncertain whether the Christian religion would survive at all. Yet it did survive, and revive.

It was from the Church that there appeared a new system of schools. Schools in monasteries had been begun for boys who were to become monks. As we have seen (p. 58), they sometimes gave the chance of education to sons of kings and nobles, and so had great influence on the outside world. But this was exceptional. Monastic schools were meant to be apart from the world. Cathedral schools grew out of the instruction given in the bishop's household. At first this was only for boys who were to become clergy. But when such schools were transferred to the cathedrals they came to belong to the whole diocese.

By the ninth century many were taking on the work of schoolmaster (Latin, *magister scholarum*). Such a man was not just a teacher, but was also 'education officer' for the diocese, and, next to the bishop himself, one of its most important figures. And, closely connected with cathedral schools, there followed in the twelfth century a revival of learning which led to a form of education which has become of world-wide influence in our own day, i.e. the rise of universities (see chapter 8).

THE CHURCH AND LOCAL LANGUAGE

The Church of the West is rightly called Latin because its Bible and liturgy were in Latin. Bede towards the end of his life became anxious to use the language of the people, and began translating St John's Gospel into Anglo-Saxon, the English of his day. He got as far as Andrew's words in chapter 6 verse 9:

'There is a lad here who has five barley loaves and two fishes. But what are they among so many?'

Then he stopped—and died (735).

This may seem an unfortunate break in the story of the feeding of five thousand. It is better to think of it as a fitting end to the story of Bede's life. One wonders if the dying man saw himself again, a little lad of seven, brought to the door of the monastery at Wearmouth (p. 99), with so little in his hands or in his head. But because he gave to Christ the little which he had, the multitude were fed.

However, the translation of the Gospels into English had to wait another two hundred years. About 950 it became customary for an English translation to be written into some manuscripts, word by word above the Latin, to help the reader explain to the congregation what the reading was about. A little later the Gospels were translated into West Saxon. German versions were beginning about the same time. A French translation of the Gospels was made later, to be read after the Latin Gospel at Mass.

The new languages of Europe had to wait so long because these languages were not regarded as 'literary', and were not looked to for serious reading. People who wanted to read books learned Latin; people who were without Latin expected to remain illiterate. King Alfred of England (849–899) was exceptional in this, as he was in so many ways: the best king and one of the best Christians England ever had. He read English as a child, learned Latin at the age of thirty-eight, and then himself translated into English Bede's *Ecclesiastical History of the English People*, a history of the world, three religious books, and part of the Psalter. He expected his lords at least to read English and to send their children to school.

Christians in the East Roman Empire, whatever nation they belonged to, were Greek in custom and language. Greek was the original language of most things Christian, and this language did not die, though it did change. For this part of Christendom, Bible and liturgy were written in an earlier form of the living language, so there was no problem of understanding. But Christians here took it for granted that other Christians might, and indeed should, want the Bible and liturgy in their own languages. It was the Greek part of the Church which was responsible for most of the early translations (see Vol. 1, p. 122).

The Christians of the East, whom many people group together as Syrians, because of their Syriac Bible and liturgy, seem to have provided translations according to demand rather than according to any set rule. In lands used to religions with Scriptures and services in a special language of religion, they have been content with their Syriac. In periods or places where the local language was demanded, they have been free to meet the demand, e.g. the eighth-century list of books translated into Chinese included both Scriptures and liturgy. The liturgical ones were the Breviary, and the Three Majesties' Praise (which is *Gloria in excelsis Deo*—see p. 50).

John of Montecorvino's translations into Mongol language, and celebration of the Eucharist in that language, must be noted as exceptional for a 'Latin' of the period, and were probably due to the example of the 'Syrians', i.e. the Church of the East (p. 86).

CHURCH BUILDING

St Paul in 1 Corinthians 3.10 compared his own work for the Church to that of a 'skilled master-builder'. The Greek word he used is *architecton*, from which comes the English word, architect. St Paul was thinking of the Church's spiritual up-building. The Church in his time had no special buildings at all, only people's houses to meet in (Vol. 1, p. 20). St Paul chose to use this parable because architecture was one of the arts in which the Romans excelled. 'Master-builders' were famous men. Examples of their work remain today in impressive ruins: bridges, aqueducts, city walls, fortresses, and, especially, public buildings, which are found throughout the Mediterranean lands, whether in Europe or North Africa. With the end of the Western Roman Empire, the time for great buildings seemed to have ended too. The barbarian invaders, now a large part of Europe's population, came from lands where people built only in wood.

Old skills are seldom lost altogether. We can best see how such skills were continued and taken up by men of Europe's new population as they became Christian, and were used in the building of churches, if we look at the life of one such builder. Fortunately Bede gives us a detailed account of just such a person, Benedict Biscop, 628–690.

The words used above, 'as they became Christians', were true of Benedict. He was the son of a Northumbrian nobleman who was baptized when King Edwin 'with all the nobles, and many of his people, came to baptism in the year 627' (see p. 31). So his family was becoming Christian when he was born.

At the age of twenty-five, Benedict asked the king of Northumbria's permission to leave court, because he felt called to the service of Christ's Kingdom. In 666, after two visits to Rome, he became a monk, and was made Abbot of the monastery of St Peter and St Paul at Canterbury. But he got the idea of founding two monasteries in honour of the same two Apostles in his own Northumbria, St Peter's at Wearmouth, 674, and St Paul's at Jarrow, 682. These were among the first stone-built churches of the English. In dedicating them, Benedict was thinking, not so much of his previous Canterbury monastery, but of Rome, where he had visited the shrines of both the Apostles.

Benedict made the journey to Rome six times, bringing back many treasures: sculpture, paintings, books, indeed a whole library (see p. 135), for his two monasteries. He even brought the Precentor of St Peter's Church, at Rome, to stay for a while and teach his monks, to sing, and to keep the festivals of the Church, as they did in Rome. For the building of the church at Wearmouth 'after the manner of the Romans of which he was fond', he brought stone-masons who had been working in France, and glass-makers who taught Englishmen their craft. Both masons and glass-makers may have belonged to Italy; their skills best flourished in Rome.

Bede tells that Benedict brought canvases from Rome, not only to beautify the walls. At St Peter's, Wearmouth, he says, a great figure of the Virgin with the new-born Jesus stretched across the sanctuary. On the north wall were pictures of the Parables, and on the south, visions from the Revelation. In the sister-church, St Paul's, Jarrow, which was built later, there were pictures showing the Old Testament fulfilled by the New: Isaac carrying the wood ('God will provide Himself the lamb,' Gen. 22.8), and Jesus bearing His cross; Moses lifting up the serpent in the wilderness (Num. 21.9), and on the cross the Son of Man lifted up (John 3.14). And Bede adds:

'So all those coming to church, though ignorant of letters, wherever they turned could gaze upon the lovely sight of Christ and His saints.'

Bede knew it so well. These two monasteries were the scene of his whole life from the age of seven (see p. 99).

Benedict's companion on his first journey to Rome was Wilfrid, a man of whom we have already read, and noted his devotion to Roman ways (see p. 35). Wilfrid was six years younger than Benedict, but the two had much in common. They met at Lindisfarne in 653, where both had gone to learn the life of religion. Both were eager to go to Rome to learn more. Both became abbots, and were famous as builders of churches in two places—Wilfrid's being at Ripon and at Hexham. The Ripon church, like Benedict's at Wearmouth, was dedicated to St Peter. Wilfrid's biographer, Eddi, describes it as:

'A church from foundations to roof built of polished stone, and supported by various pillars and colonnades.'

Pillars were a feature of Roman buildings, and these may have been brought from the ruins of the Roman town of Isurium, which was called by the English (and is still called) Aldborough (i.e. Old Town) only seven miles away. So this church may have owed some debt, not only to Roman influence but to Roman materials.

To sum up, Benedict, and his companion Wilfrid, show us:

1. that some Roman skills may have been learned by the use of Roman materials;

2. that builders who practised Roman skills (building with stone, and making glass for windows) could still be hired from abroad;

3. that, more important than the ruins of Roman work scattered over Europe and North Africa, was Rome itself, which remained as the greatest inspiration, example, and source of everything needed for the building, furnishing, and conduct of the churches.

THREE CENTURIES OF
SPECIALLY GREAT CHURCH BUILDING,
1050–1350

From church building in the seventh century, we must now turn to a surprising development in the eleventh. About the year 1050 there came a burst of new life throughout western Europe, which expressed itself in the building of great churches. It lasted for three hundred years, and resulted in hundreds of churches which remain today Europe's chief architectural glory. Nothing like it had happened before. Nothing like it has happened since.

The achievements of the men who lived in these three centuries, 1050–1350, remain a mystery and a marvel, but we can note three conditions which helped to make them possible: peace, wealth, and full development of architectural skills.

1. *Peace*: The raids of the Northmen (see p. 36), western Europe's last pagan invaders, had ended by the year 1000. Under the previous system of divisive feudalism, every landowner had been able to call out his private army (p. 77). Now organized states were beginning to arise in Europe, especially in France and Germany. Thus hope of an end to civil war began to dawn.

2. *Wealth*: Trade was increasing, cities were growing, and there were more men in more places who were able to think beyond the need for food, clothing, and shelter.

3. *Full development* of architectural skills: this is the most important condition, which we must examine in greater detail.

With new opportunity for building, new master-builders did appear. They had taken over much knowledge from the ancient world, and by trial and error had also learned some new skills. With new skills they developed new styles.

These new master-builders were practical men, not just drawing plans for a building but at work there on the building site. Their training had been practical: they had learned by doing. They began as unskilled workmen, served their apprénticeship, and qualified as masons. Each of them went on shaping stone and setting it in its place till he was accepted by master-masons as one of their number. He had to become well known as a master-mason before he could be given the contract for one of these great churches.

Men with such skills were in great demand, from the south of France to the north of England, from eastern Germany to Spain. They did not limit themselves to their own country. Indeed they hardly knew which country was their own. They were not always travelling, because the building of a cathedral or an abbey would take many years, and for those years they would settle in that one place.

Their coming changed the life of the place. They engaged crowds of workmen to quarry the stone and to move it, to dig the foundations, and erect scaffolding. So there were new jobs, new transport, new skills. And in their lodgings they talked far into the night about life in other lands, making the townsfolk feel as if they too had come to belong to a wider world.

Early churches had been of the kind called *basilica* (Greek for 'royal hall'). This word was later used of any hall, but especially of the rectangular style of church, entered through a porch on the west, with an apse (half-circle) for the altar on the east. Some churches were two-room rectangles, consisting of a sanctuary to the east, and a nave, the length of the church, to the west, with an arched dividing wall. But now the shape of larger churches, cathedrals, and minsters, was fully 'cruciform', i.e. cross-shaped, with the sanctuary for altar and clergy, nave, and transepts (cross-parts) between.

In the period of great church building, the architects made little use of classical columns. They wanted to build to greater height, and, to be free from fire, they wanted to build roofs of stone. Weight from above can break a beam, but it strengthens an arch by pressing the shaped stones together. So within their stone walls they built great pillars, or piers of stone, with round arches from wall again. And they studied the art of stone-vaulting, known to the Romans, which can be described as continuing a round-arched roof for the building's whole length. It was a demanding task. For example, the Abbey Church at Cluny in Burgundy was rebuilt in 1130. Its vaulted roof was one hundred feet high and three hundred feet in length. Both outer walls and inner

7.6 About the year 1200 builders began to use pointed arches, and stone ribs fanning out from the pillars to bear the weight of the roof-vault, so walls could be lighter and windows larger. Fan-vaulting in Ely Cathedral is regarded as one of the wonders of medieval building.

piers must be built in massive strength to support so heavy a roof. So churches of this type, of which Durham Cathedral (p. 100) is a good example, give a sense of being enclosed, and shut off from the world, like a fortress on guard against its evil. This sort of architecture, distinguished by thick walls, stone piers, and round arches between, is called Romanesque, which means 'developed from the Romans'.

Sculptors added ornaments to the top of piers and arches—flowers and beasts, crosses and angels. Pictures had been painted on the walls of churches, as we have seen, from the time of Benedict Biscop (p. 104). But now more and more complex scenes were carved in stone, and then painted over in reds and blues and gold. The abbot of Moissac, a small town in the south-east of France, wanted a scene carved over the west door of his Abbey, which was newly built in the year 1115. He made one of the biggest demands ever made on a sculptor. He read out Revelation 4.2–8, the description of God's glory, and asked the sculptor to carve it in stone: God on His throne beneath a rainbow, and before Him a sea of glass like crystal. Twenty-four elders look up adoringly, enthroned, crowned, each holding a harp and a golden bowl for the prayers of the saints, which means God's people. Four living creatures are always moving around the Almighty, a lion, an ox, a man-faced figure, and a flying eagle, for ever going round, and round, and round (see p. 100).

If we read the passage we may feel that with so much piled-up imagery it is difficult to see the picture even in one's imagination. It would be still harder to paint it in colour. It must have seemed impossible to carve it out of a single piece of stone. But the abbot had said, 'I want them to see that when they come into my church.' And there it is, all of it, the most perfect example of Romanesque sculpture.

About the year 1200 came another advance. Instead of the rounded arch, builders began to use the pointed arch. If you break a semicircle into two and join the pieces together in a point, you not only increase the height of the window, you change the impression given by the arch. Instead of feeling that weight is pressing down from above, everything points upwards. The builders had found that walls need not be so massive in order to hold up the roof. If you stand under a stone vaulted roof, you will be reminded of standing under an umbrella—from the centre there are 'ribs' going out in every direction. In the roof it is these stone 'ribs' that bear the weight of the roof, smaller stones being used for the spaces (like the cloth of the umbrella) in between. The weight of the roof, instead of pressing directly downwards, could be carried by arched supports in the walls, and the walls in general could be made lighter. This meant that greater space could be given to windows. Strength within the walls could be increased by buttresses, and, where necessary, by 'flying buttresses', which added support from ground level right up to the roof.

This style of architecture, with pointed arches, and walls which give more space to windows, was given an unfortunate name, 'Gothic', meaning 'barbarous'. This was at a time, from the sixteenth century onward, when men regretted that the styles of Greece and Rome were no longer being used. But some of the world's most beautiful buildings resulted from the fact that Christian church architects did depart from Greek and Roman ways and develop new ideas in building, and not just building with stone, but building with stone and glass. The stained glass of these great churches was something that was unknown before. To pictures painted on the walls, and pictures carved in stone and standing out from the walls, it adds pictures which glow and flash in the sunlight, and which, like the arched windows which contain them, were meant to point heavenwards.

STUDY SUGGESTIONS

WORD STUDY

1. What do the following Latin words mean?
   (a) *forum* (b) *viaticum* (c) *trivium* (d) *quadrivium* (e) *magister scholarum*
2. Explain briefly what the following terms mean:
   (a) basilica (b) vaulting (c) rib-vaulting (d) transept (e) buttress
3. Why were some of the larger churches in the Middle Ages called 'minsters'?

REVIEW OF CONTENT

4. Why in Europe today do we sometimes find large stone or brick churches in places where there is only a small village population to use them?
5. 'The priest's chief task was the ministry of Word and Sacrament' (pp. 96-97).
   (a) What other tasks did a local priest usually have in the Middle Ages?
   (b) Which, if any, of these does a priest *not* so often have today, and why?
6. (a) How were the clergy trained for their service of the Church?
   (b) Why was it not possible for them to be educated in ordinary schools?
7. In what ways was the education of Willibrord and other Church leaders like that of Samuel in the Old Testament?
8. (a) Who was the builder of two monasteries in Northumbria

dedicated to the same two Apostles as a monastery in Canterbury, and when did he live?

(b) Where did he chiefly get his ideas for building these churches?

(c) Who and what did he bring to England to help add to the beauty of these churches?

9. Wilfrid was another church builder of the same period. Where were the two most important churches that he built?

10. (a) What were the three chief conditions which made possible the great development of church building in western Europe in the 300 years from AD 1050 to 1350?

(b) What were the usual stages of a master-builder's career at that time?

(c) 'The coming of master-builders to build a cathedral or abbey changed the life of the place' (p. 106). In what ways did it change?

11. In earlier centuries most large churches had been built in the classical Roman style, and sometimes even with Roman materials. What new styles and skills were introduced by church architects and builders in the 11th and 12th centuries?

12. What were the chief differences between the Romanesque and the Gothic styles of church architecture?

DISCUSSION AND RESEARCH

13. (a) What were the 'seven works of mercy' which the clergy would urge their people to undertake in the Middle Ages?

(b) Who is chiefly responsible for these 'works of mercy' in your own country today?

(c) Do you think that these works should always be the responsibility of Christians, or can others do them better? Give reasons for your answer.

14. 'The church was usually the best building in the place' (p. 96). How far is this true of places which you know today? Give examples. Can you suggest reasons for your answers?

15. (a) For what purpose was stained glass chiefly used by medieval cathedral builders?

(b) Do you think it is as important today for church builders to use stained glass and painting, as it was in the Middle Ages? Give reasons for your answer.

16. 'When St Paul compared his own work to that of a skilled master-builder (1 Cor. 3.10), he was thinking of the Church's spiritual upbuilding. The Church in his time had no actual buildings at all' (p. 103).

To what extent, if at all, do you think that a Church's spiritual life is benefited by the building of beautiful churches as a setting for worship?

17. Describing the paintings in Benedict Biscop's church at Jarrow, Bede noted that 'all those coming to church could gaze upon the lovely sight of Christ and His Saints'.

   In later times many churches were despoiled of their paintings and sculpture by earnest Christians who believed such embellishments to be 'idolatrous'. What is your opinion?

18. In what different ways does the Church give men 'training for Church service' (p. 98) in your country?

CHAPTER 8

Schoolmen and Universities

We have seen that, surprisingly soon after the end of the Dark Ages (500–1000), there came three centuries (1050–1350) of great church building. Churches built in that period are the pride of western Christendom today. It may seem still more surprising that in the first two of these three centuries (1050–1250) there was also a surge of intellectual life which produced a succession of great theological teachers. The greatest of these was one who in his lifetime was called 'the Angelic Doctor', .and whose work Roman Catholics of the twentieth century receive as 'the classic expression of the Christian Faith'. These theological teachers are known as 'the Schoolmen', and the greatest of them is St Thomas Aquinas.

They are called 'Schoolmen' because they belonged to the 'schools' or colleges which had begun to flourish at that time in some of the monasteries, and in still more cathedrals (p. 101). Just before the year 1200 some of these centres of learning, as we shall see, began to develop into universities. These men were the products of this movement, and the movement was produced by the men. Both these things are true.

In this chapter we shall consider five of the most important Schoolmen. We shall also note another stimulating event; this was when scholars in the Latin West began to take a new interest in the ideas of the Greek philosopher Aristotle (382–322 BC). And we shall end with a section on the rise of universities. The five Schoolmen are Anselm, Abelard, Peter Lombard, Albert the Great, Thomas Aquinas.

ANSELM (1033–1109)

Anselm was the first important theologian to become Archbishop of Canterbury. He was Italian, born at Aosta on the southern slopes of the Alps. As a young man he travelled to Bec in Normandy, to a small monastery made famous by Lanfranc, a fellow-Italian, who taught there. In 1066 Duke William of Normandy became King William I of England, and many Normans followed him there, including Lanfranc, who became Archbishop of Canterbury. At Bec, Anselm took his place as theological teacher, and later became abbot. Anselm visited Lanfranc in England, where he became known and admired by the clergy. When Lanfranc died in 1089, they chose Anselm to succeed him, but King William II knew that Anselm would oppose his attempt to control

112

Church appointments and affairs. In 1093, however, the king, who was gravely ill and had the four years' vacancy on his conscience, consented. Anselm would have preferred to continue in scholarly quiet at Bec. He wrote:

'I trusted my own strength and wit to keep me where I wanted to be. But God has proved stronger and craftier than I.'

He found it hard to imagine the king and himself pulling the same way. He was sixty.

'It is like yoking an untameable bull to a weak sheep'.

Conflict with the king did twice drive Anselm into exile. But he continued to stand for the rights and liberties of the Church and to act for its reform. He also continued his theological writing.

One great subject in which all the Schoolmen were interested is expressed in St Augustine's words: 'Understand so that you may believe; believe so that you may understand.' Which do we put first, faith or reason? Anselm saw no need for conflict between the two. What the Christian faith teaches is an essential part of a reasonable view of the universe and of life.

Anselm's most famous work has a title of three short words, *Cur Deus Homo* (Latin for 'Why God Man', i.e. 'Why did God become Man'). What Anselm wrote in this book is of permanent value to the Church.

We saw that in the Early Church (Vol. 1, p. 141) theological thought in the Latin West was practical. Theologians were concerned less with the inner life of God than with the actual life of man, i.e. man as a sinner and how he may be forgiven. Jesus spoke of Himself as giving His life as 'a *ransom* for many' (Mark 10.45 and 1 Tim. 2.6). 'Ransom' is the price to be paid for release of a slave; it was a familiar thought in Roman society, which depended upon slave labour. From earliest times Christians had discussed this saying of Jesus, and had asked themselves to whom the 'price' was paid. The answer seemed to be, 'to the devil'.

Anselm said 'No'. He saw that it was blasphemy to think that the Devil could make such a demand from God. There are not two supreme beings, only one. We must think of God alone.

The word which Anselm used to explain the question is *satisfaction*, which means 'payment of what is due'. This is a term used in Roman law, but it describes a moral obligation which is basic to society of any kind. For example, as we have seen (p. 74), feudalism was based upon ownership and use of land. *Feu* means 'fee', i.e. payment for services given. A feudal system is one in which land is received from one's lord for services given; services are due to one's lord for such lands received. This whole idea lay behind Anselm's conflict with the king. Anselm agreed that the fact that the archbishopric possessed much land made him the king's 'man'; for these possessions he would do 'homage'. The difference between them was that, as archbishop, Anselm claimed at the same time to be the king's spiritual father, but the king would not acknowledge this.

In using the word 'satisfaction', Anselm was thinking of moral obligation in terms of a feudal society. Man owes God service. Sin means that instead of serving Him, man has rebelled. The difference between service and rebellion is as great as the difference between heaven and hell. Anselm uses these words to describe how great the difference is which man has to make up:

'Such *satisfaction* none can make but God.
And yet the debt is owed by none but Man,
So the God-Man had come to pay it.'

ABELARD (1079–1142)

Peter Abelard was born near Nantes in western France, of an aristocratic and pious family. He early showed a love of learning. As a student he often caused trouble by being more clever than his teachers, and in Paris himself became the most popular of teachers, with a huge following of students. They loved his extravagant statements which shocked his hearers to silence—a silence that ended in a burst of applause. Such statements as:

'You must not believe something because God has said it—but because your reason is persuaded that it is true.'

Abelard's best-known work, *Sic et Non* (Yes and No), was a book intended for beginners. In it he deals with questions about science, ethics, and religion, giving as answers quotations from Scripture and from the Church Fathers. But the quotations show that there is no easy answer; yes *or* no. Always there is more than one answer: yes *and* no. In other words, there is room for a variety of opinions, and need for independent thought. Abelard had been educated in the new Aristotelian logic (see p. 115), and his book was meant to stimulate logical reasoning. Yet Abelard would claim that he did not exalt reason above faith. He too believed that they belong together.

With regard to the saving work of Christ, Abelard took what Anselm said (not that God is in conflict with the Devil, but that there is *only* God), and urged his hearers to go one step further. He did not see two principles in God, love wanting to forgive, and law demanding satisfaction. He saw only love. Abelard taught that the saving power in the death of Christ is that it shows us, sinners, how far the love of God will go to save us, and that it is this love which moves us to repent.

Many, including the great and good Bernard of Clairvaux, who wrote:

'Jesu, the very thought of Thee
With sweetness fills my breast'

thought Abelard too bold, not only because of this teaching, but in much
else. However, concerning the love of God, there is the great passage
in 1 John 4.8,10; 3.16:

'God is love,
In this is love, not that we loved God
but that He loved us and sent His Son . . .
By this we know love,
that He laid down His life for us.'

And, borrowing Abelard's own title, *Yes and No*, we may ask, If this
Scripture says 'Yes', can anyone say 'No'?

PETER LOMBARD (1100–1160)

Peter the Lombard was born near Milan, in Lombardy, hence his name.
After studies at Bologna in Italy and Reims in France, he taught at the
Cathedral school in Paris. He is famous for his book, *The Sentences*,
which is in four parts:

1. God, the Trinity, God's attributes, Predestination,
2. Creation, Man, Sin, Free Will, Man's need,
3. Redemption,
4. The Seven Sacraments: Baptism, Confirmation, Eucharist,
   Penance, Extreme Unction, Ordination, Marriage.

The book is a treasury of quotations from the 'Fathers', as early Christian writers were called. At that time books were scarce and costly. For
many people the only way to get another book was to borrow one and
then spend days and nights copying it. Here was a book with selections
from a whole library. The Bible and *The Sentences* were often the only
books which a theological student owned.

ALBERT THE GREAT (1193–1280)

Albert was born in Germany, and studied in Italy. He became a Friar of
the Dominican Order, and a famous lecturer at Paris University, and
later at Cologne. His interest was in science, and he made full use of the
works of Aristotle as an aid to Christian thought about the universe
and the life of men. Some of these works had only recently been rediscovered in the Latin West.

NOTE: THE RECOVERY OF ARISTOTLE'S LOGIC, SCIENCE, AND ETHICS.
This is a subject worth more than a passing mention, as it shows how

Christian influences were passed from west to east across the world and back again, in most unexpected ways.

We saw (p. 64) that Syriac-reading Christians of the Church of the East, through their religion, had inherited much of the learning of the Greeks. In positions of influence in Persia, they became the civilizers and teachers of the Arabs who conquered Persia, so that by the year 850 the Muslim Empire which superseded Persia became the leading civilization. Much of Aristotle's work had not been preserved in the Latin West. It came to the knowledge of scholars in this period because, having been translated from Greek into Syriac, and from Syriac into Arabic, it was now translated from Arabic into Latin. Later, more translations were demanded, and were made directly into Latin from the Greek.

All this was welcomed by such scholars as Abelard and Thomas Aquinas. Aristotle's logic contributed to the liveliness of Abelard's lectures, which drew such crowds. One of the exciting features of Thomas's theology was that he could accept the Greek view of the universe found in Aristotle, without letting it disturb the Christian view of God and of man revealed in the Scriptures.

THOMAS AQUINAS (1225–1274)

Thomas was born in a village near Monte Cassino in central Italy, the youngest son of the Count of Aquino, hence his name.

When Anselm, the first of our five Schoolmen, was made archbishop at the age of 60 in the land of a tyrannous king, he called himself, 'a weak old sheep'. When Thomas Aquinas, the last of the five, was a young student, big, broad, and with little to say, he was nicknamed by fellow-students 'the dumb ox'. His silence must have been because his thoughts were deep. When he did come to speak and to write he showed a clear mind and a gift for clear expression. He was born to privilege. With his family connections and his native abilities he could have chosen any department of life and become a great figure there. He was closely related to both the Emperor, and the king of France. As a boy he was sent to school at the neighbouring Benedictine monastery of Monte Cassino, where the Abbot was his uncle.

But while he was at Naples university, completing his study in arts, he came to know his calling: he must give himself to be a leader of Christian thought, and to do this he must join the Dominicans, the Order of Brothers Preachers. His family opposed this and confined him in one of their castles for fifteen months, but he escaped and did become a Friar. He studied theology at Paris under Albert the Great, and went with him when he moved to Cologne. Later he taught in several Italian cities, including Rome, was appointed adviser to three Popes, and did his most influential teaching in Paris.

Thomas Aquinas wrote much. Besides his theological works, he wrote commentaries on the Gospels and Epistles, Isaiah, Jeremiah, the Psalms, and Job. On quite a different line, he wrote the services for the Festival of Corpus Christi (Latin for 'the Body of Christ', meaning the Eucharist). This festival was newly added to the Church year in 1264 (its day is the Thursday after Trinity Sunday). The reason for adding this festival was that Maundy Thursday, the day of the Eucharist's institution, was also 'the night when He was betrayed' (1 Cor. 11.23), and so was considered too sad a time to express Eucharistic joy. For the services Thomas wrote joyful Latin hymns, including:

'O Bread to pilgrims given,
O Food which angels eat,
O Manna sent from heaven,
For heaven-sent natures meet . . .

Jesus, this feast receiving,
We Thee unseen adore,
Thy faithful word believing,
We take and doubt no more.'

His most famous work is the *Summa Theologica* (Latin for 'theological system', i.e. systematic theology). It took him nine years to write. It is all-inclusive, and deals with every question raised by the enquiring mind. It is set out in three parts:

1. God—His existence, nature, attributes; the Trinity; God in Himself before all things; and God as known in creation and providence;

2. Man—his fallen nature, yet a nature able to be redeemed; his vices and virtues, law and grace;

3. Christ as God-Man—the Redeemer, the Way back to God. (This is the shortest section. Thomas died leaving it unfinished.)

Dealing with the basic question of faith and reason, Thomas gives great scope to reason, holding that even apart from revelation, men may arrive at belief in God, His eternity, oneness, creative power, and providence. Full Christian belief, in the Trinity, God's actual work of creation, the fall, the Incarnation, the life everlasting—these are not unreasonable; reason may show their probability, and may justify their acceptance. But the ground of our belief in them is not reason but revelation, through the Scriptures, and the Fathers of the Church. These we accept by faith, which is an act, not of our intellect, but of our will, and is therefore a moral decision.

With regard to Aristotle's teaching, Thomas did more than Albert his teacher. He not only understood Aristotle, but positively admired

8.1 The greatest of the Schoolmen was Thomas Aquinas, who in his lifetime was called 'the Angelic Doctor'. In Fra Angelico's painting of him, done about a century later, he looks more like the 'dumb ox', as his fellow students nicknamed him when he was 'young, big, broad, and with little to say'.

his powers of argument, his method of scientific enquiry, and his emphasis on man as a rational being.

As for the doctrine of the atonement, Thomas combined Anselm's view with Abelard's: that Christ made satisfaction for the sins of men, and that His doing so is what moves men to love Him.

UNIVERSITIES

The gradual, almost unnoticed, growth of a university may best be illustrated from Paris. *Universitas* was not the name first used, but *studium generale* (Latin for a place for 'study of every kind').

The city of Paris had an exceptional number of teachers. We saw that as early as the eighth century the school at the monastery of St Denys, to the north, was famous enough for the ruler of France to send his two sons there (see p. 58). Within the city, the cathedral of Notre Dame had its school, and to the south the churches of St Victor and Ste Genevieve each had one. In Abelard's time, and partly because of his attractive personality, students flocked to the city.

The teachers or masters, many of whom were not Parisians nor even Frenchmen, felt it necessary to combine together, just as at this time members of different crafts or trades were combining in 'guilds', in order to protect their rights. Their connection with the Church freed these teachers from control by the city. But connection with the Church placed them under the bishop, who, through the cathedral chancellor, or education officer, was the authority who gave or withheld the right to teach.

Masters of more advanced studies wished to be free from all local interference, so they appealed to the Pope, who took them under his own protection. This meant that there was no authority but these masters themselves to fix standards for teachers and students. They had become a new institution, a *studium generale*, a university. Fortunately Popes continued to regard universities as 'rivers of knowledge which feed and fertilize the universal Church' (Pope Innocent IV, 1243). Such independence became the accepted right of universities, and most of them were founded by charter from the Pope.

Paris grew to be a city full of student youth. We noted the over-statement of Rabban Sauma, the monk from China who visited Paris in 1287, and gave their number as 30,000 (see p. 83). Probably it was not more than 4,000 or perhaps only 3,000. But the total population of Paris at that time may have been only about 50,000 and 3,000 in 50,000 is six per cent. They would seem many indeed.

Being young and vigorous, the students would be the group which made its presence felt. Students came to Paris from every province of France, from many nations of Europe, from as far east as Syria and

Egypt. The city fully recognized the university's importance. When the king of France visited Paris, the rector of the university was there to read a Latin address of welcome, his colleagues with him in their gowns and hoods. On the death of a rector the city gave him the burial of a prince.

There were of course occasions when students were noticed in the city's life because they interrupted its peaceful flow. Street fighting often broke out, one side 'town' (i.e. the townspeople), the other 'gown' (i.e. students in their academic dress). Students were often up to some mischief, especially at night: setting a trail of gunpowder to go off under the night-watchmen's feet, or emptying over the city guard, or policemen, the cart which each night collected the city's filth.

UNIVERSITY STUDIES

University studies were divided into four faculties: theology, law, medicine, arts; arts being by far the biggest. The visitor from China mentioned above was impressed by the university's studies, as well as its numbers:

> 'They study ecclesiastical and profane learning, that is to say the interpretation and explanation of all the Holy Scriptures; and science, that is to say philosophy, rhetoric, medicine, geometry, arithmetic, and the knowledge of the planets and stars.'

Here he does get most of the content of theology and arts (see p. 99). And he is right in placing theology first. 'Queen of the sciences' it was often called, and was given an honoured place in every university, and especially distinguished in Paris. How different it seemed to that monk from China, from places where Christians were a small minority!

Most of the teachers and most of the students of a medieval university were clergy, because throughout the Dark Ages learning had been preserved and passed on by the Church. The clergy were no longer the only educated people, but they were the best educated.

Students came up to a university from the age of thirteen onwards, with seven years of *trivium* and *quadrivium* to complete (p. 99). Much of the early work, for a boy of thirteen for example, would today be done at school.

At the end of the arts course a man became 'Bachelor of Arts'. 'Bachelor' was a word first used of military, not academic, qualification. It meant a young knight serving under a senior knight's banner, not yet having one of his own. Academically it meant a man who had specialized in one department of knowledge, but was not yet fitted independently to teach it. Later he became 'Master', which meant that the university's chancellor gave him the right to teach.

Beyond the arts course, a student might choose to go on to theology, or law, or medicine, which were, as we now say, post-graduate courses. But we must not think of post-graduate theology as training which the Church required for its pastoral ministry. Only a few parish priests had been to university. The equipment of most was simpler—Latin from the grammar school, and at the cathedral school some acquaintance with parts of the *trivium* and *quadrivium*, to which were added, by the bishop or one of his more capable clergy, exposition of the Bible and some practical training.

UNIVERSITY BUILDINGS AND ORGANIZATION

Universities had begun with almost no buildings of their own. All through the Middle Ages Paris never had a hall big enough to hold all its students. Lectures were given from church pulpits. Students sat, and wrote, on the floor. No dormitories were provided. Some teachers found room for a bed or two about their own house. Students slept wherever they could find a bed. Many worked, some as copyists of books (there were jobs for hundreds in the book trade in Paris), many at more servile tasks, in order to stay and study at the university.

One of the earliest hostels in Paris was given by a London merchant, who, returning from pilgrimage in the Holy Land, was sorry for 'poor, deserving students' in the city, and provided a house called 'Eighteen' because it had beds for that number. Later there were several colleges where students could live. The most famous of these, originally for Masters of Arts who were advancing to theology, was the Sorbonne, called after its founder (in 1253) Robert de Sorbon, and now Paris's chief centre of theological learning. He was chaplain to the king of France, Louis IX, who is rightly named St Louis. Robert de Sorbon also left this wise advice to students:

'You will need each day:
a time-table kept,
attention fixed,
memory trained,
notes taken,
discussion with your fellows,
prayer to God.'

The university of Bologna in Italy began in conditions which contrasted with those in Paris. Paris was famous for arts and theology, Bologna as the finest law school in Europe. In Bologna most of the staff were local citizens: it was the students who, after art studies in other countries, came to Bologna for law. As foreigners it was they rather than the teachers who felt it necessary to combine to protect their rights. As might be expected of men on their way to become lawyers, they combined most effectively. So it was from the student end that a university began to take shape. A committee of students hired each teacher, fined him if he was late in starting his lecture, or late in stopping it, allowed him only one day's holiday if he wished to get married, and often forgot to pay his salary. This went on until the city fathers interfered and set up an organization more worthy of a *studium generale*.

In 1167 King Henry II of England, because of a quarrel with the king of France, ordered English teachers and students at Paris to return home, and by 1185 Oxford had its own recognized *studium generale*, and went on developing colleges, much on the lines of Paris. In 1209 some students from Oxford moved to Cambridge, which was already a centre of learning, and which in turn became a university by 1233.

Between 1200 and 1400 twenty-five universities were founded in Europe:

in France, ten,
in Italy, seven,
in England, two,
in Germany, four,
in Spain, one,
in Portugal, one.

Scotland added two more by 1451.

In our own day the growth of universities has been both quickened and extended, beyond all previous expectations, and has become an important factor in the life of every country of the world.

On the surface it may seem that the state has taken the lead which in the Middle Ages belonged to the Church. But closer examination will show that in this modern period of universities' world-wide development, the way for many universities has been prepared by Christian schools and colleges, and Christian-educated teachers have played a part worthy of being compared with that of Christians of the medieval Church.

STUDY SUGGESTIONS

WORD STUDY

1. What was a *studium generale*?
2. What is the origin of the word 'university'?

REVIEW OF CONTENT

3. (a) Who were the 'Schoolmen' and why were they given that name?
   (b) Who was the greatest of them, and what two very different nicknames was he given during his lifetime?

STUDY SUGGESTIONS

4. At what period did universities begin to develop?
5. In this chapter, five of the most important Schoolmen have been studied.
   (a) Give the dates of their births and deaths?
   (b) What other things did they share, besides being theologians?
6. (a) For what reason did Anselm oppose King William II, and what were some results of his opposition?
   (b) What was the most important book which Anselm wrote?
   (c) How did he interpret Jesus's statement about Himself, as giving His life 'a ransom for many' (Mark 10.45 and 1 Tim. 2.6)?
7. (a) Of what nationality was Peter Abelard, and where did he chiefly teach?
   (b) What was the title of Abelard's best known book?
   (c) Why did Bernard of Clairvaux say that Abelard was 'too bold'?
8. (a) What does the name 'Lombard' mean?
   (b) What sort of book was Peter Lombard's 'the *Sentences*'?
9. (a) What was Albert the Great's chief interest?
   (b) Of which other great Schoolman was Albert the Teacher?
10. What events in the 11th and 12th centuries led to renewed interest in the teaching of the Greek philosopher Aristotle?
11. (a) What sort of family background did Thomas Aquinas have?
    (b) In what ways, if any, were his experiences like those of Francis of Assisi?
    (c) In what ways were they different from those of Francis?
    (d) What was his most famous writing? Give details of some of his other writings.
    (e) Summarize briefly Thomas Aquinas's teaching about reason.
12. (a) By what authority were teachers in the earliest universities controlled?
    (b) 'Most of the teachers and students at a medieval university were clergy' (p. 120). Why?
    (c) At about what age did students enter university in the Middle Ages, and how did they live?
13. How did the phrase 'town and gown' arise?
14. In what ways were the beginnings of the university of Bologna different from those of the university of Paris?

DISCUSSION AND RESEARCH

15. (a) What did Peter Abelard mean by saying that in questions of science, ethics, and religion there is always more than one answer: yes *and* no? Do you think he was right? Give reasons for your opinion.
    (b) What was Abelard's teaching about the love of God? Compare it with the teaching of your own Church on the subject.

123

16. (a) Into what four 'faculties' were university studies divided in the Middle Ages?
    (b) Into what chief faculties are university studies usually divided today?
17. 'We must not think of post-graduate theology as training which the Church required for its pastoral ministry' (p. 121). What sort of educational training *did* parish clergy have in the Middle Ages? What sort of educational training do pastors have in your country today? Do you think it is adequate? How could it be improved?
18. Find out what part, if any, the Church has played in the setting up of universities or university colleges in your country or region today. What other agencies have been concerned in the setting up of modern universities?
19. By what authority are the universities in your country or region controlled? By what authority do you think they *should* be controlled?
20. (a) For what is Robert de Sorbon chiefly remembered today, and what 'wise advice' did he give to students?
    (b) What additions to this advice, if any, would you give today?
21. In 1963 a report to the Commission on World Mission and Evangelism of the World Council of Churches stated: 'True excellence in theological study will only grow in a Christian community.' What is your opinion?

CHAPTER 9

Popes in Power:
The Idea of Christendom

We now return to a subject begun in Chapter 5: 'Franks and the Pope'. In that section (p. 61), we imagined Alcuin reading to Charlemagne from Augustine's *City of God*, and telling him about God's plan for government on earth as described in Augustine's book about the 'two cities': the city of this world, and the heavenly Jerusalem. 'Alcuin encouraged Charlemagne to think that in God's scheme, in which the Pope of Rome held spiritual power and the Emperor of Rome held worldly power, he, Charlemagne, had a part.'

AUGUSTINE:
THE CHURCH AND THE KINGDOM OF CHRIST

Augustine, in his book, gave a picture of the Kingdom of Christ as something which already exists in this world wherever the Church shares power with the State. This is how he interpreted Revelation 20, about the Devil's being bound for a thousand years, while the souls of the martyrs live and reign with Christ for a thousand years. Notice that he discouraged literal-minded people, who use the Revelation to calculate when the end of the world will come:

'It says a thousand, meaning all the years of this age . . . the very fullness of time, because a thousand is the cube of ten . . . The binding of the Devil was not only when the Church began to expand to other and still other nations. It goes on still, and shall do to the end of time. For now too men turn to the Faith from that faithlessness in which the Devil bound them. While the Devil is bound, the saints are reigning with Christ. It cannot mean that Kingdom of which it is said, "Come, O blessed of my Father, inherit the Kingdom prepared for you from the foundation of the world" (Matt. 25.34). There must be another Kingdom far different, where in a different way His saints now reign with Him. . . . "The son of Man will send His angels and they will gather out of His Kingdom all causes of sin." Can this mean that Kingdom where there is nothing to offend? No, it means this Kingdom which is the Church . . . Even now is the Church the Kingdom of Christ, and His saints now reign with Him, but not as they shall reign.' (*City of God* XX, 8, 9)

Chart 2: TIME LINE AD 1000-1500

Year (AD)	LATIN CHURCH	GREEK CHURCH	SYRIAN CHURCH
1000			
1050	1046 Emperor Henry III 'cleanses' papacy 1049–71 Four reforming Popes 1073 Pope Gregory VII excommunicates the Emperor 1077 The Emperor a penitent at Canossa 1081 The Emperor sets up a rival Pope 1085 Pope Gregory VII dies in exile 1096–1291 Eight Crusades	1054 East–West Schism 1071 Seljuk Turks destroy Roman army at Manzikert and capture Emperor	
1100	1109 Anselm dies	1099 First Crusade victorious: Jerusalem recaptured	
1150	1142 Abelard dies 1160 Peter Lombard dies		
1200	1198–1216 Pope Innocent III, 'Vicar of Christ' 1209 Call of St Francis	1219 Francis preaches to Sultan of Egypt	
1250			

126

Year (AD)	LATIN CHURCH	GREEK CHURCH	SYRIAN CHURCH
1250	1274 Thomas Aquinas dies		1259–94 Kublai Khan Emperor at Khanbalik (Peking)
	1292–1303 Pope Boniface VIII: papal claims fail in face of French and English nationalism	1287 Sauma ambassador to Constantinople to promise Mongol alliance in Crusade	1281 Mark (Chinese monk) Catholicos of the East
1300	1305–78 Papacy at Avignon	1291 Last Crusade loses Acre	1294 John of Montecorvino reaches Peking
	1315 Ramon Lull, martyr at Bugia		
	1329–84 John Wycliffe		1321 Four Franciscans martyred near Bombay
1350			1336–45 Tamerlane depopulates Central Asia
	1378 The Great Schism		
1400			
	1417 The Council of Constance		
	1431 The Council of Basle		
1450	1447 Nicholas V, Renaissance Pope	1453 Constantinople falls to Ottoman Turks	
	1450 Gutenberg develops printing at Mainz		
	1484 Bartholomew Diaz to Cape of Good Hope		
	1492 Columbus discovers New World		
	1493 Rodrigo Borgia as Pope		
1500	1497 Vasco da Gama: Portuguese displace Moors in parts of Asia		

So Augustine passed on the idea of the Kingdom of Christ as something which is already here, or at least already begun, in Christendom. In order to understand this idea, we need to understand just what Christians in the Middle Ages meant when they used this word 'Christendom'.

NICHOLAS I (855–867):
THE POPE AS HEAD OF CHRISTENDOM

Western Christians of the Middle Ages had no doubt that the Bishop of Rome held a central place in Christ's Kingdom. They thought of him always as 'vicar', i.e. representative, of St Peter, who in the New Testament is first of the Apostles (Matt. 10.2), the rock on which the Church is built (Matt. 16.18). The Bishop of Rome was unique in so many ways that it was easy for legend to add more. For example, in about 750, in the Dark Ages, just before the brief brightness of Charlemagne's reign, someone in France produced a document called the *Donation of Constantine*. These are the words supposed to be decreed by the Emperor Constantine:

'As the earthly and imperial authority belongs to us,
so we have decreed that the holy Roman Church . . .
the most holy See of blessed Peter should be gloriously
exalted . . . and should be first of the four Great Sees,
Antioch, Alexandria, Constantinople, and Jerusalem, as
over all the Churches of the holy Roman Church . . . should be
chief of all bishops, and that all provision for the worship
of God and the establishing of the Faith should be ordered
according to his judgement.'

The document goes on to say that Constantine gave to the Pope rule over all Italy, including Rome, and 'the provinces, places, and states of the regions of the West'.

In the Middle Ages scholars were less critical than they are today. The *Donation of Constantine* was accepted as history, and was not shown to be a fiction till the fifteenth century. The document is not historically true, but it is related to history. When it was written, that was how things appeared.

The Pope had for a long time been acting as an independent ruler of Rome, and of territory around the city (see p. 59). In 753 he went to Paris to crown Pepin, as if the kingdom of France, i.e. a large part of the 'states of the regions of the West', were the Pope's to give. The only ongoing unifying power which could be called 'Roman' was by then to be found, not in the Empire, which in the West had ceased to be, but with the Pope.

Those who drew up the *Donation of Constantine* were stating their belief that western Europe still had a central authority, no longer the Roman Empire, but 'the holy Roman Church'.

About the year 850, and probably in France again, a bigger collection of documents appeared, called the *Decretals*. It contains letters of early Popes, all false; rules drawn up by Church councils, most of them genuine; and papal letters from the fourth to eighth centuries, some genuine but thirty-five false. Those who put together these *Decretals*— some of them genuine decisions of Church councils—were showing that canons (i.e. fixed rules) protected a bishop if he or his people were oppressed by the ruler of the country, or by the ruler of that Province of the Church (i.e. by his archbishop). These canons would be enforced if he appealed over his oppressors to the head of the whole Church, the Pope.

Nicholas I was Pope at this time, and he accepted without question these documents which seemed to support his power, because this was what he believed. Indeed, this was how, as Pope, he determined to behave. The Pope, as head of the Church, would be head of Christendom, i.e. he would rule over all the lands where the Church had power. Nicholas summed up the message of all these *Decretals* in the words, 'That which the Pope has decided is to be observed by all.'

By the Treaty of Verdun, 843, the great Empire which Charlemagne once ruled had been divided by his grandsons into three parts, roughly corresponding to present day France, Germany, and a long corridor between them (eastern France and northern Italy). The three parts were ruled respectively by Charles (France), Louis (Germany), and Lothar I. It was at this point that France and Germany began to think of themselves as separate nations (see map 4, p. 69). Thus there was no all-powerful Emperor in Europe, no one whom Nicholas I felt he need fear at all—but he was a courageous man.

In 860 Lothar II, who had succeeded his father as ruler of eastern France and northern Italy, wished to have his marriage annulled, and accused his wife of incest. The fact was that he wished to marry one of his mistresses. Louis of Germany, Lothar's uncle, agreed, and two archbishops shared in proceedings by which the marriage was declared null. The disowned wife appealed to Pope Nicholas. He sent his officials to make enquiries, and when he found that the officials had been bribed, dismissed them, and set up a court of enquiry in Rome. The Pope announced his findings: the innocence of the queen was established; both archbishops were deposed; and King Lothar must receive back his wronged wife. Lothar protested, and his uncle Louis felt he must defend the archbishops who had been their allies. So Lothar and Louis marched on Rome. But uncle Louis was taken ill. In the end he submitted to Pope Nicholas's decision, and Lothar had to do the same. He took back his Queen.

THE CLEANSING OF THE PAPACY (1046)

Lack of an all-powerful Emperor gave a strong Pope like Nicholas I the opportunity to show what the Pope as head of Christendom might do. But in the next century lack of effective government, with no strong ruler to enforce law and order in Rome itself, or to ensure a properly chosen succession of Popes, was to bring the Papacy to the depth of humiliation.

The rule of the Church was that a bishop should be chosen by the clergy, accepted by the people, and consecrated by bishops within the province. The choosing of the Bishop of Rome was a special case, and there were often exceptional happenings.

Just before and just after the year 1000, there were violent uprisings of people suffering under the feudal system throughout the West. Among the institutions which they threatened, was the Papacy. They complained that instead of the Roman clergy choosing the Pope, and responsible Christian laymen solemnly approving the choice, the palaces of the Pope and the Papal State which he ruled, the Patriarchate of the West itself, had come to be regarded as the property of one noble family in the city of Rome. This was the family of the Count of Tusculum, and one member of that family after another had become Pope. The first of them had the virtue of being able to keep order and hold robbery in check. The second had been governor of Rome, and so knew much of local affairs. The third, in 1033, was a mere boy in his teens, but he already had so many vices that there was no room in him for any virtue at all. He took the name of Benedict IX. A later Pope wrote of him:

'Benedict—the name means *blessed*. But after being made Pope, his life was so shameful, foul, and *accursed*, that I shudder to mention it.'
(Pope Victor III, 1086)

So far from accepting Benedict, some of the people of Rome made a plot to assassinate him, and if they had been successful they might have done God service. In 1044 they drove him out and accepted Silvester III. But after a few weeks Benedict was back, and he was able to expel his rival. However, finding the Papacy a burden, he sold it to an older member of his family, who was his godfather, and who took the name Gregory VI.

Buying the Papacy is surely the most serious example of the sin of 'simony', the name used in the Middle Ages for buying and selling of spiritual things, as did Simon the magician in Acts 8.18. It is clear however that Gregory was doing evil in order that good might come. He wanted to become Pope so that he could reform the Papacy. With him was a young admirer, Hildebrand, whom he made his chaplain, and who was to spend his life in such reform.

The need for reform was not yet fully shown. Benedict changed his mind. He would not give up what he had sold. So in Rome there were now three Popes at once, Benedict IX, Silvester III, Gregory VI. This was too much. The people of the city sent an appeal to the Emperor Henry III. He came to Rome in 1046, and declared all three deposed.

Gregory VI, the best of the three, went off to retirement in Cologne, and Hildebrand stayed with him till his death in 1048. After that Hildebrand spent some months in Worms as an eager student of Church law. When the Emperor nominated his own cousin as Pope—he was to take the name Leo IX—Leo discovered this young man at Worms and invited him to join those who planned to reform the Church.

REFORMING POPES

The first action of Leo IX (1049–1054) was to refuse to enter Rome in pomp as Pope designate. He came barefoot, dressed as a pilgrim. That is what he considered himself till chosen and accepted in Rome.

Of his five years as Pope, Leo stayed in Rome altogether for about six months. The rest of the time he spent in being the active 'head' of the Western Church. He travelled over Italy, France, and Germany, reinvigorating the Church, improving its discipline, encouraging archbishops and bishops to get on with the Church's real work: the care of souls. He appointed cardinals and advisers from lands beyond Italy.

In Leo's papacy the rift between Rome and Constantinople became complete. The old struggle for leadership, and new theological disputes, ended in open schism in 1054.

Hildebrand had much to do with the nomination of another reformer, who took the name Nicholas II (1058–1061), looking back in admiration over two centuries to the great Pope Nicholas I. He presided at a council in 1059 which freed the Papacy from its political connection with the city of Rome and its disorders. The Council decided that neither the people of Rome, nor the local nobility, would in future be allowed any part in the choice of a Pope. The choice was to be made by the cardinals. The Pope need not be a Roman, nor need he come to Rome to be enthroned before exercising his authority. Thus the Pope was made more representative of the whole Church of the West. The same Lateran Council of 1059 forbade lay investiture, i.e. the placing in office by a *secular* ruler of one who is to be bishop or abbot (see p. 132). (Kidd, *Documents* III, pp. 117–119.)

It was in 1073 that Hildebrand, who for nearly twenty-five years had been one of the powers behind St Peter's throne, was called to ascend it. Strangely enough, his being chosen as Pope was not according to the rule of 1059, i.e. by the cardinals. At the funeral of Pope Alexander II (1061–1073) a shout sounded through the Church, and soon everyone was shouting, 'Hildebrand! St Peter chooses Hildebrand.' The cardinals hastily consulted together and then announced him Pope. He took the name Gregory VII. (Kidd, *Documents* III, pp. 123–124.)

THE INVESTITURE CONTROVERSY

This phrase is used for the dispute between the Church and rulers of state, about the right of emperors, kings, or other lay princes, to appoint bishops or abbots. To 'invest' means to clothe, i.e. to put on a man the robes belonging to his new appointment. What actually happened when a bishop or abbot was appointed was not the putting on of robes, but the giving of a ring for his finger, and a pastoral staff (i.e. shepherd's crook) into his hands, with the words: 'Take the Church'. The emperor, kings, and other lay princes claimed the right to do and say this, and then to receive 'homage', i.e. a promise of faithful service, from the bishop or abbot so appointed.

As we have seen, in 1059, under Pope Nicholas II, lay investiture was forbidden. Pope Gregory VII repeated this order in 1075—and many times afterwards. It was much more than a question of ceremonial. It may well have seemed fundamental to the welfare of a kingdom. Great offices in the Church were of concern to a king. Throughout Europe the Church was the greatest of all owners of land. Bishops and abbots ruling over Church lands had power over a large proportion of a kingdom; and some of them ruled over as large a single area as did a count or duke. Then again, while a countship or a duchy was *inherited*, a bishop or an abbot was *appointed*. That meant that the king could choose his man, and so strengthen his own following.

Those who wanted to reform the Church believed that lay control of Church appointments was wrong. They included such practices under the sin of 'simony' (p. 130). (Kidd, *Documents* III, p. 128.)

Pope Gregory VII was among the most extreme of the reformers. He did not believe that there could be two powers in God's scheme of things, a spiritual power and a worldly power. For him there was only one: the spiritual power was all that mattered. Among his letters there has come down to us a list of his beliefs about the Papacy which he must have made about the year 1075. Here are some of them:

The Pope can be judged by no one.

The Roman Church has never made a mistake, and never will.

The Pope alone can depose a bishop or restore him, call Church councils, give authority to Church laws.

The Pope can depose Emperors, and loose subjects from their allegiance.

All Princes should kiss his feet.   (Kidd, *Documents* III, pp. 129–130)

Pope Gregory did not make these claims for himself, they were claims for Christ's Kingdom. Gregory, like Augustine, believed that the Kingdom was here already, in the Church, and that the kingdoms of this world were meant to become the Kingdom of our God and His Christ.

The clash came between King Henry IV of Germany and Pope Gregory VII, over the appointment of a new archbishop of Milan. Milan was an important city, and its bishop would have many responsibilities in the State besides his work in the Church. The king wanted to have his own men in such positions, so he chose his man and invested him: 'Take the Church'. The Pope wrote to the king, pointing out that he had recently forbidden such an investiture, and added:

'Saul was robbed of his kingdom when pride caused him to despise the words of Samuel.'

At that very time Henry was requesting that, as King of Germany, he might now, by the Pope's coronation, be advanced to Holy Roman Emperor, as his father had been. And here was the Pope warning him that instead he might lose his crown as king. Henry was furious. He wrote:

'Henry, no usurper, but king by God's holy decree, to Hildebrand, not Pope, but a false monk.'

And he ended his letter with a warning:

'Condemned by the judgement of all our bishops, and by our own judgement, come down! Give up the Apostolic see, that another may ascend to the chair of St Peter. I, Henry, by the grace of God king, with all my bishops, say to you, Come down! Come down!'

The reply of the Pope was to excommunicate and depose King Henry IV. The Pope made his solemn declaration in a prayer to St Peter, in whose place he was acting:

'Blessed Peter, Prince of the Apostles . . . hear me thy servant, whom thou hast brought up from a child, and saved from the hands of wicked men . . . Of thy grace I have received from God authority to bind and to loose (Matt. 16.19). Relying therefore on this trust . . . and because King Henry, son of the Emperor Henry III, has risen with unheard of pride against thy Church, I withdraw from him the government of the whole German and Italian kingdom; and I release all Christians from the bond of their oath (of loyalty), and I forbid anyone to obey him as king . . . that all may know that "thou art Peter, and upon thy rock the Son of the living God hath built His Church, and the gates of hell shall not prevail against it".' (Kidd, *Documents* III, pp. 130–131; Bettenson, *Documents*, pp. 144–145.)

We may wonder if these high-sounding words would carry much weight when there were few armed men for a Pope to move against a king. However, a wide kingdom like that of Germany and Italy, containing many princes, dukes, counts, and other local rulers, could easily be divided. Saxony was always ready to rebel. Many of the dukes would not be sorry to see the king's central power reduced. Many of the bishops would be afraid to share with the king his excommunication. Henry IV soon realized that his supporters were becoming fewer. He must act without delay. And his first action must be, at any cost, to make peace with the Pope.

CANOSSA (1077)

Pope Gregory was on his way from Rome to Germany, and was staying at Canossa in north Italy, in the castle of one of his most devoted friends, the Countess Matilda of Tuscany. King Henry took his wife and child, and in the depth of a severe winter crossed the Alps, having a path cut for him through snow and ice. And this is how the Pope reported Henry's coming to the castle as a penitent:

'Without any show of hostility or insolence, he arrived in the town with a small retinue. For three days he stood in misery before the castle gate, having taken off his royal robes, barefoot, dressed only in a woollen garment. With many tears he implored the aid and consolation of our apostolic pity . . . At last, overcome by the urgency of his grief, and the prayers of all present, we loosed the bond of our excommunication, and received him into the bosom of holy mother Church.' (Kidd, *Documents* III, pp. 131–133)

In this act we see Pope Gregory more as a priest than as a statesman. Here was a penitent and he must give him absolution. It was not a statesmanlike act. The Saxons complained that the Pope had failed them. The rebel dukes went on to elect one of themselves as their new king, but they had less confidence in the triumph of their cause.

As for Henry, by 1080 he sent envoys to the Pope suggesting that he should excommunicate the rebels. He knew that the Pope would refuse, but he wished now to pose as a defender of law and order, against aggression encouraged by the Pope. He got a council of bishops to nominate Wibert as Pope, and in 1081 marched to attack Rome. Henry besieged the city for three years, and when at last the gates were opened to him and his Germans, the Pope retreated to the fortress of St Angelo on the river Tiber and held out there.

Meanwhile Henry enthroned his supposed new Pope, who crowned him as Emperor.

Then came the Normans (i.e. North Men). They had been invading

9.1 'Innocent III, the Pope of highest achievements, kept the movements of revival inside the Church.' (pp. 136–139)

This thirteenth-century painting of him is in the lower church at Subiaco, where Benedict (seen at the left) first established a monastery.

and settling in south Italy for years, and Gregory had promised to recognize their conquests in return for aid. The Normans saved the Pope but sacked Rome, destroying far more than Goths, Huns, and Vandals had done in the 'bad old days'. Gregory's allies took him with them to Salerno, where in 1085 he died, saying sadly:

'I have loved righteousness and hated inquity (Ps. 45.7),
Wherefore I die in exile.'

This civil war, which had started because of the dispute about how a bishop should be invested, did not end till 1122. This same dispute brought Anselm, Archbishop of Canterbury, into conflict with King William II of England (see. p. 113), and England was sixteen years ahead of Germany in settling it, by a similar compromise, but without any fighting.

In Germany the compromise was this: the Emperor (or king) agreed to allow 'canonical' election, i.e. election (of bishop or abbot) by those who had the right according to Church law. The Pope agreed that such election could take place in the emperor's (or king's) presence—so he might have some influence upon it. The emperor (or king) should not give the ring and staff; those were from the Church, symbols of spiritual authority. But a bishop or abbot should do homage to his prince for the lands which were entrusted to his rule.

For Germany and Italy, a life-time of civil war had delayed the progress of civil government, and progress towards national unity.

There have been many different estimates of Pope Gregory VII. Some people may be content to accept his own estimate, and quote the pessimism of his dying words. Some will admire his courage, believing that the Church should have a bold programme for changing the world. Some will condemn him, judging that the Church should not make use of worldly weapons.

It may be best to go back, earlier than Pope Gregory, to that 'maker of Latin Christianity', St Augustine, and with him boldly claim: 'Even now is the Church the kingdom of God.' We can live and serve the Church in that spirit; while at the same time we add the saving clause: 'His saints now reign with Him, *but not as they shall reign.*'

POPE INNOCENT III (1198–1216):
THE POPE OF HIGHEST ACHIEVEMENTS

Pope Innocent III is usually thought to show the greatest glories of the medieval Papacy. He made the same high claims for his office, with one slight change—and advance—in the wording:

'Kings rule each in his own kingdom.
Peter rules over the whole earth.
The Lord Jesus Christ has set up one order over all things:
All should bow the knee to the Vicar of Christ.

Innocent here continued, as Gregory had done, to use the title, which had been traditional for so long, 'Vicar of Peter'. With both Gregory and Innocent, the thought had really changed to 'Vicar of Christ', as Innocent expressed it.

Innocent made his claims to power less fiercely than Gregory, partly because he was more of a statesman, and so less of a fighter; and partly because there were fewer to oppose, so he had less need of fighting.

He was the son of a noble family in Rome, with the best education that a youth could enjoy—theology at Paris, then law at Bologna. His uncle was Pope. He himself was made a cardinal at thirty, and Pope at thirty-seven. And just four months before that, the Emperor, who had been the greatest power in Europe, suddenly died, leaving a child of three his heir—and the Pope to be his guardian. What a chance!

The only one to oppose him, as in Germany Henry IV had opposed Gregory VII, was John, king of England. John refused to accept the Pope's nominee for Archbishop of Canterbury, and in 1212 the Pope deposed him, and ordered the king of France, England's traditional enemy, to invade. Of all England's kings, John was the most lamentable. He had set both barons and people against him. Now he kneeled before the threatening Pope and received back his kingdom as the Pope's gift, for which he did homage—an action which Englishmen hated to remember. As a result, anti-papal feeling began in England, a country which from the days of Pope Gregory the Great had done so much to exalt the Papacy. 'We are the seal of his Apostleship,' Bede had said (see p. 24).

We must note two of Pope Innocent's achievements: the Lateran Council of 1215, and the recognition of the Friars.

Innocent summoned to the Council archbishops and bishops, abbots, priors, heads of monastic orders, kings, and rulers. They were *ordered* to come to Rome, not invited. Of bishops alone, over four hundred came. So many came that, at the opening meeting, an aging archbishop who stumbled was trampled to death in the throng.

It was the most important Church council of the Middle Ages. It defined teaching about the Eucharist, and added the instruction:

'Let every one of the faithful once a year make confession to his own priest . . . and reverently receive the sacrament of the Eucharist, at least at Easter.' (Kidd, *Documents* III, p. 155)

It ordered that in every Province a council should meet once a year. It urged the importance of preaching, since spiritual food is necessary for

9.2 'In the clash between King Henry IV of Germany and Pope Gregory VII,
Henry realized that he must make peace with the Pope at any cost.' (p. 134)
An engraving in Foxe's *Book of Martyrs* shows how Henry came to Canossa as a
penitent to beg Gregory for release from excommunication.

salvation. All bishops, it said, should be preachers, but if they lacked the necessary time or learning (which in future they must not lack), then they should appoint suitable preachers and confessors. Cathedrals and other greater churches should have among their clergy a master appointed to teach poor scholars and make no charge. Every province should have a theologian to train its clergy. Moral standards, especially of the clergy, were discussed and regulated in some detail.

One of Pope Innocent III's great virtues was that, scholar and statesman as he was, he recognized the spiritual value of people far different from himself. When groups of humble laymen, believing themselves called to a life of poverty, began to call themselves 'Friars', i.e. brothers, and went about preaching among the poor, hearing their confessions, and tending lepers, Innocent encouraged them. He welcomed this movement of religious enthusiasm, and made room for it, unconventional though it was. In this way he kept this movement of 'revival' inside the Church, instead of driving it into 'heresy' outside. Both Franciscan and Dominican Orders of Friars were established in his time (see p. 83). This was one of Pope Innocent III's greatest achievements, and a great achievement of the Church of the West in this period.

POPE BONIFACE VIII (1294–1303): PAPAL CLAIMS QUESTIONED

Pope Boniface was of a family which had produced several Popes, including Innocent III. He was a lover of learning, and was associated with the founding of more than one of the early universities (see p. 119). He made claims as great as those of any of his predecessors. One sentence will be enough:

> 'It is altogether necessary to salvation for every human being to be subject to the Bishop of Rome.' (Bettenson, *Documents*, pp. 159–161; Kidd, *Documents* III, p. 186)

Boniface came into conflict with the kings of both France and England. Not that these kings stood together. On the contrary, they were enemies, and he might easily have played off one against the other. In 1296 the Pope condemned King Philip IV of France for taxing clergy and Church property. In one of the king's defences to the Pope, came these words:

> 'It is the right of kings, with the advice of their parliament, to provide all things necessary for defence of the realm, according to the command: "Render to Caesar the things that are Caesar's".'

A long struggle then began, with so many conflicts that the Pope was ready to excommunicate Philip and depose him. At the same time the

Pope interfered with King Edward I of England, who was claiming the throne of Scotland too. Boniface ordered Edward to stop his invasion, as Scotland was in a special way under papal protection. In 1301 the English parliament sent him a long statement. At the centre of the statement are these words:

'The kings of England do not, and ought not to, answer concerning their rights before any judge, ecclesiastical or civil.' (Kidd, *Documents* III, pp. 182–184)

In 1303 King Philip took action against the Pope. He hired a band of armed men to surround the Pope's house at Anagni, the small town in Italy where he was born. They made him their prisoner, but the men of the town soon came to his rescue, and took him back to Rome. The Pope was seventy, and suffered both in body and in spirit. A month later he died, and the period of great papal claims to political power came to an end.

Times were changing, and this was a sign of the change. People were beginning to have a feeling of 'nationality' and of pride in national independence. These were new factors in the situation. An authority like the Papacy, which claimed to be supra-national, or indeed universal, might have to make its claim in a new way.

STUDY SUGGESTIONS

WORD STUDY

1. What is 'simony', and why is it called that?

REVIEW OF CONTENT

2. 'Western Christians of the Middle Ages had no doubt that the Bishop of Rome held a central place in Christ's kingdom'. (p. 128) Why did western Christians believe this?
3. (a) What was the *Donation of Constantine*?
   (b) In what way did it give support to the power of the Pope?
4. What were the names of Charlemagne's grandsons and how and when did they divide France between them?
5. In what ways did Nicholas I begin to show how a strong Pope could influence the actions of worldly rulers?
6. (a) What was the rule of the Church for choosing and consecrating bishops?
   (b) What event had led to the neglect of this rule around the year 1000 AD?
7. (a) How did it come about that in 1044 there were three men all claiming to be Pope?
   (b) How did the Emperor deal with the situation?

8. (a) Name the three 'reforming' Popes who were in office between 1049 and 1073.

(b) What new rules for the choosing of Popes were made by the council held in 1059?

9. (a) What was the custom of 'lay investiture'?

(b) Which two Popes passed rules forbidding the custom?

10. (a) List some of Pope Gregory VII's beliefs about the Papacy.

(b) In what way did his ideas about power in Church and State differ from those of Alcuin?

(c) 'Pope Gregory did not make these claims for himself' (pp. 132–133). For whom did he make them?

11. Describe in your own words the 'clash' between Pope Gregory VII and King Henry IV of Germany. In doing so, say what happened at Canossa, and how in the end Henry got himself crowned emperor.

12. Describe how the same clash between the Church and the king or emperor was settled in (a) England, and (b) Germany.

13. (a) What change did Pope Innocent III make in the wording of his claims for papal power?

(b) What special 'chance' to increase papal power did he have?

14. (a) Which king opposed Pope Innocent III?

(b) What did he do that hurt the pride of his subjects?

15. (a) List some of the rulings which made the Lateran Council of 1215 'the most important Church council of the Middle Ages'.

(b) The Lateran Council was one of Pope Innocent III's achievements. What was his other most important achievement, and why was it important?

16. (a) Which was the Pope whose interference in the affairs of France and England brought to an end a period of great claims to papal power?

(b) Which kings were reigning in the two countries at the time, and which of their actions did the Pope oppose?

DISCUSSION AND RESEARCH

17. 'Augustine passed on the idea of the Kingdom of Christ, i.e. "Christendom", as something which is already here, wherever the Church shares power with the State'. (p. 125)

(a) Do you agree with this idea? Give your reasons.

(b) Where, if at all, is 'Christendom' to be found in the world today?

18. (a) Which Churches still believe today that the Bishop of Rome holds a central place in Christ's Kingdom?

(b) What is the teaching of your Church on this subject?

(c) What is your own opinion about it?

19. (a) How can historians judge whether or not a historical account or document is genuine?

    (b) For what reasons might a writer of history forge documents or produce false accounts of earlier events?

20. Find out in what countries today customs similar to that of 'lay investiture' (see p. 132) are still practised, and in what ways, if any, they differ from the original custom.

    Do you think that such practices are a good thing for the Church? Give reasons for your answer.

21. Find out what rules the different 'episcopal' Churches have today for choosing their bishops. Which sort of rule do you think is likely to be the best?

22. Some Christians condemn Pope Gregory VII for relying on armed force. They say that the Church should not make use of worldly weapons. What is your opinion?

23. (a) What Christian agencies today, if any, claim the right to interfere in national and international affairs?

    (b) Give examples of any action taken by the Church in opposition to the rulers of any state.

    (c) Do you think such action is justified?

CHAPTER 10

Movements for Reform

MONKS—
A MOVEMENT OF SPIRITUAL RENEWAL

Towards the end of Volume 1 in the chapter called 'The Coming of the Monks', came these words (p. 146): 'The passage in the Gospel which has most often moved men to seek a way of more complete devotion to Christ, is: "If you would be perfect, go, sell what you possess, and give to the poor . . . and come, follow me" (Matt. 19.21).' And again, 'People left the worldly Church for the more devoted life of the monks.' Monasticism began as a movement of spiritual renewal.

Volume 1 ended with the year AD 500, which was about the time when Benedict made his crowning contribution to the movement by becoming a monk. We consider him in detail here, rather than in Volume 1, because throughout the Middle Ages bursts of new religious life generally took a monastic form. A leader would gather a few followers, and start a new community of monks. And Benedict was so well remembered, and so highly thought of, that in many cases it was not so much a *new* community that such leaders formed, as one which turned back to Benedict and his Rule, with fresh determination to keep it.

BENEDICT OF MONTE CASSINO (480–540)

Benedict had been sent as a boy in his teens for education in Rome, but he was so shocked by the immorality of the city that he went off to live by himself in a cave in a steep valley about thirty miles away. The place is called Subiaco (Italian for 'below the lake'). The village got this name when it housed the Emperor Nero's workmen, who put a dam across the valley and made a lake for the pleasure gardens which Nero loved. In this Emperor's garden in Rome, Christians were burned as torches in the year 64—see Vol. 1, p. 69)

Followers gathered around Benedict, and in 529, after they had been living in small groups, each under a leader, Benedict built a monastery on Monte Cassino. Monte is Italian for 'mountain', and the monastery stands high up, half way between Rome and Naples (map 3B, p. 32). Benedict remained there till his death and burial about 543.

Benedict's ideal for his monks was a community which elected its own abbot (from the Syriac *Abba*, for 'Father'), and then obeyed his fatherly rule. Monks were to be admitted as 'novices', i.e. on trial for a year, and then took vows for life, living in the community without any possessions of their own. Theirs was a simple life, busy and disciplined, bound together by what Benedict called the *Opus Dei* (Latin for 'work of God'). This was a scheme of eight daily worship periods, coming at intervals of about three hours throughout the day and night. Each worship period included prayers, psalms, and Bible reading (see chart).

THE WORK OF GOD		
Name (from Latin)	*Meaning*	*Approximate time*
The Day Hours	'Seven times a day I praise thee'	Psalm 119.164
Lauds	'Praise'	dawn
Prime	'First'	6 am
Terce	'Third'	9 am
Sext	'Sixth'	12 noon
None	'Ninth'	3 pm
Vespers	'Evening'	dusk
Compline	'Completion'	bedtime
The Night Office	'At night I rise to praise thee'	Psalm 119.62
Mattins	'Morning'	2 am

Prime, Terce, Sext, None: Jewish reckoning, with day starting at 6 am

Chart 3: *Opus Dei*—the 'Divine Office', or scheme of daily worship which St Benedict laid down for his monks

THE RULE OF ST BENEDICT

Benedict's Rule contained detailed instructions for his monks—even telling them how to sleep, with one candle burning in the dormitory, clothed and belted so as to be ready, but 'without the knife in the belt, lest they hurt themselves while sleeping'. The instructions are detailed but concise, only about 12,000 words. In some ways Benedict's was a typically Roman contribution to the life of the Church. There was little that was new—new ideas were more often Greek than Roman. Benedict owed much to earlier monks; Pachomius, Basil (see Vol. 1, pp. 148–152), and others; and an especial debt to *The Rule of the Master*, which was compiled not long before his own. But Benedict contributed an emphasis on discipline, and that is Roman. He said that that was the purpose of his Rule:

> 'That in the effort of obedience you may find the way back to Him from whom you strayed in disobedience . . . renouncing your own will, to serve Christ the Lord, the true King, taking up the mighty and glorious weapons of obedience.'

Along with discipline, Benedict made another contribution, which was not Roman but Christian, and that was a tenderness, a deep concern for his men, which ran throughout his work:

> 'We intend to found a school to train men in the service of the Lord, in which we shall not make rules too strict and heavy . . . If we show some severity, do not take fright and run away. The entrance to the path of salvation must be narrow, but when you make progress in the life of the Faith, the heart expands and speeds with the sweetness of love along the path of God's commandments.'

The Rule was strict. Obedience was to be 'without delay . . . above all, no murmuring for any cause, by any word, or gesture.' But those who ruled the monks were told to consult with them on important matters, and not with the seniors only.

It is often to the younger that the Lord reveals what is best. Prayer, as we have seen, was to cover the day, and even break the night in two. Of the night prayers, at 2 a.m. in unheated buildings, the Rule says:

> 'When the brothers rise, let them gently encourage one another, because the sleepy ones are apt to make excuses.'

And of private prayer, Benedict advised 'little and often', knowing our weakness:

> 'Our Lord says that we shall not be heard for our many words (Matt. 6.7). So our prayer should be brief and pure, unless it is prolonged by the inspiration of God's grace.'

When a monk did wrong the punishment was to be shut out of the fellowship, and left to do the daily duties alone. Even then, Benedict added:

> 'The Abbot must show care towards the brother who offends. Let him send senior monks, as it were secretly, as companions, to comfort him, lest he be overwhelmed by too much sorrow . . . The Abbot must remember that he is there to take care of weak souls, not to tyrannize over the strong. He must not lose one of the sheep entrusted to him.'

Benedict planned a well-proportioned life for the monks. Of the twenty-

The organization of the Dominicans and that of the Franciscans are similar, but Dominic called for sound learning as a guard against heresy, while Francis sometimes spoke as if the Friars were better without books.

10.1 In a fourteenth-century painting of St Dominic in Naples, he holds a bundle of manuscripts.

10.2 The Franciscans 'like the birds, would possess nothing for themselves' (p. 151). A sixteenth-century painting of Francis at Subiaco shows the simple habit and rough rope girdle worn by Franciscan Friars.

four hours, his men got eight hours for sleep; seven for manual work—
'idleness', he says, 'is the enemy of the soul'; four for study; four for the
daily services; one for meals. In the eight daily services they went
through the Psalms every week. In time they would know many of them
by heart. And in these services they read most of the Bible every year.

Benedict wrote as though progress along this narrow, but broadening,
path was easy and assured (see the second quotation above). The ideal
was continually held up before the monks. The word 'chapter' came to
be used for a whole body of monks meeting together, and 'chapter
house' for the place where they met, because every day they did meet
to hear a *chapter* of the Rule read aloud before other business was done.

Such a high ideal must always have been hard to achieve, and harder
still to maintain. In the ninth century the Northmen robbed and burned
monasteries all round Europe's northern coasts (see p. 36). Feudal disorders in the tenth century (p. 74) disturbed every sort of institution,
including monasteries. The sinful practice of simony (p. 130) meant that
there were abbots who enjoyed a monastery's broad lands, instead of
taking care of weak souls. But throughout these troubled times the Rule
of St Benedict remained all over the west as *the* monastic rule, and as an
ideal unchallenged (Bettenson, *Documents*, pp. 161–179).

CLUNIACS (910)

Berno was abbot of a monastery in France which stood for strict following of St Benedict's Rule. So many young men were applying to become
monks that Berno decided that a new monastery was needed, and he
asked the Duke of Aquitaine for a house. Unfortunately the house he
asked for was the Duke's favourite hunting lodge at Cluny (map. 3B,
p. 32). However, Abbot Berno was sure that the housing of his
monks mattered more to Almighty God than the housing of the Duke's
dogs, and he told him so. The Duke, William the Pious, was not
difficult to persuade. To found a monastery meant that the founder
would be remembered in the monks' prayers for generations to come.
So the monastery was founded at Cluny in 910. Its church, rebuilt
in 1130, was at that time the largest in Europe (see pp. 106, 108).

Following the Rule of St Benedict, the monks of Cluny from the
beginning elected their own abbot. The Duke was anxious that the
building and lands should not be seized for any other purpose, so he
placed the monastery directly under the Pope. Thus Cluny had a better
chance than most monasteries of being left undisturbed either by the
State (e.g. being seized or taxed by any future duke or other ruler), or
by the Church (e.g. being interfered with by local bishops). Cluny,
enjoying these reforms, became a centre of reforming influences.

Odo, the second abbot of Cluny, travelled widely in France and

Italy. He persuaded many monasteries—including even Monte Cassino and Subiaco, the places of Benedictine monasticism's earliest beginnings—to follow Cluny's example.

Compared with earlier Benedictines, the monks of Cluny (known as Cluniacs) made the eight daily services longer and more elaborate. Since these services took more of the monks' time, farm work was more and more handed over to servants. Not that monks at Cluny felt superior to humble toil. Odilo, a monk of noble birth, came as a novice and was kept busy cleaning lanterns and washing floors. He became abbot in 994. He was a man of learning, and with artistic taste, but also of great piety. He increased the music in the services, and adorned the church with marble. The pious side of his character is shown by his being responsible for starting the observance of All Souls' Day (November 2, following All Saints' on November 1). It is a day of prayer for all the departed, and it is said that the reason why he got it added to the calendar was that so many people wanted a share in this good man's prayers.

The independence of Cluny, with its free election of abbots, and special protection from the Pope, was praised and talked about. There were other evils waiting to be put right, for example civil war. The idea of the Truce of God (see p. 74) began at Cluny. And Cluny strengthened the campaign against simony (p. 130) and other abuses in the Church. In 1150 there were over three hundred Cluniac monasteries. The abbot of Cluny had become head of a large 'family' of monasteries, with a prior under him in every daughter house, and all of them standing for high ideals of the Church, the Church which they believed was to rule over the whole earth.

CISTERCIANS

Just before the year 1100, a man named Robert became the leader of a new but very small monastic movement in another part of France, at Citeaux near Dijon (see map 3B, p. 32). The monks there had begun by living in huts made from tree branches, but now moved into more permanent buildings. They were followers of the Rule of St Benedict, but aimed at a return to great simplicity of life. Their clothing was made of undyed cloth, not black like that of other monks. They were often called 'the white monks', but their appearance was only a greyish white. Instead of the elaborate prayers and music of the Cluniacs, their daily services were simple, their crucifix was of wood, their robes not silk but cotton. They reduced the length of the services, and spent more time in silence. And as they opened more monasteries, they chose sites for them in the wild, in country to be cleared and tilled by their own labour. They had bands of lay brothers, who were allowed more food and sleep than themselves, so that they could do this hardest work; but these also, though not able to read, had a part in the daily worship.

These monks of Citeaux were like the Cluniacs in being linked into a 'family' of monasteries. Each one was visited once a year by the abbot of the mother house, or his deputy. In many parts of Europe are places where Cistercians (the word is made from the Latinized form of Citeaux), were the first to clear the forest or drain the fen.

Bernard (1090–1153) is the most famous Cistercian. He came of a noble Burgundian family, and when he joined, he brought with him five of his brothers and nearly thirty friends—such was his power to influence men. A contemporary record says:

> 'Mothers used to hide from him their sons, wives their husbands, men their friends,'

—lest he should persuade them to leave the world and become monks. At the age of twenty-five Bernard became abbot of the fourth Cistercian house, at Clairvaux. He became a great reforming and purifying influence in the Church, and so, chiefly through him, did the whole Cistercian Order. He was far more of a spiritual power than the Popes of his time.

Bernard said that he had often experienced the presence of Jesus:

> 'I have never known at what moment He came or went, but I have known that He was there. How, I know not.'

The hymn, translated from Latin into many languages, 'Jesu, the very thought of Thee, with sweetness fills my breast', even if it is not by him (as most hymnbooks say it is), certainly came from one of his company, and breathes his spirit.

THE COMING OF THE FRIARS

The most important movement of spiritual renewal in the later Middle Ages was the coming of the Friars—the Dominicans and the Franciscans.

The Friars seemed nearer to the life of Jesus and of the first Christians, because, unlike most monks, they were not shut away from the world, but in it. And they did not come, as many monks and most nuns did, from the more privileged classes. They were poor, or in sympathy with the poor. And all of them were ready to beg their bread (as the rule of St Francis said), 'without a blush of shame, since the Lord made Himself poor in this world for our sakes'. Their influence was immense. As trade and wealth grew, towns were growing. The poorest people, living in huts which they built outside the town walls, were not provided for by the ordinary parish system. There was a need for help, and the Friars came to fill it.

DOMINICANS: ST DOMINIC (1170-1221)

Dominic was a Spaniard, born of a noble family who lived near Osma in Castile. He became canon of the cathedral there, and then was sent to Provence, an area in south-west France, to work among the Albigenses, sometimes called the *Cathari* (Greek for 'the pure'). These people were a heretical sect revived from the early centuries. They combined Christian teaching with Persian ideas about matter being evil. Their leaders were called 'the Perfect', and they did live lives of great strictness, in contrast with the lax and mostly ignorant Christian clergy of that area. The Church was trying to suppress these heretics by force, but Dominic was sent to convert them if he could. His missionaries, he knew, must excel in holiness, love, and powers of persuasion.

In 1215 Dominic opened a house in Toulouse, and he and several colleagues lived there in community. The name 'Friars (i.e. Brothers) Preachers' was later suggested for them by Pope Innocent III, and they still use this name more often than 'Dominicans'. The work spread and grew, and by 1277 they had four hundred houses.

The organization of the Dominicans and that of the Franciscans were similar. Areas of work were divided into 'provinces', each under a head —the Franciscans calling him 'minister'. Each had a Second Order, for women, and a Third Order for both men and women in ordinary life who accepted their ideals and lived in simplicity and faithfulness.

The founders of the two Orders were opposite in one way. Dominic had found in Provence ignorant priests, and this made him call for sound learning, as a guard against heresy. Study was a first duty for a Dominican. Francis, however, had a fear of learning, thinking that it might spoil the simplicity of his Brothers. He sometimes spoke as if they were better without books—even a prayerbook.

In some ways the two Orders grew more closely together. Dominic in 1218 attended the 'General Chapter' (see p. 147) of all the Franciscans. And in 1219 the Dominicans too became devoted to 'the Lady Poverty' (i.e. they refused all personal possessions), and became a 'mendicant' (begging) Order. The Franciscans, after their Saint's death, found that they had to provide training for their Friars. When Universities began to be established (pp. 112-119), both Orders saw the opportunity for work among youth, and took it. Of the Schoolmen, Albert the Great and Thomas Aquinas were Dominicans (p. 116), Grosseteste (p. 154) was patron of the Franciscan house in Oxford. Both Franciscans and Dominicans became great missionary Orders. We have already followed some of the Friars in their adventures across the world (p. 55).

FRANCISCANS:
ST FRANCIS (1181-1226)

In chapter 6, p. 84, we saw something of St Francis's call in 1209; the Second Order for women, and Sister Clare, the first of them; the Third Order for people in ordinary life; and Francis's love of nature, his gaiety, and his acceptance of the world mission. We shall be reminded of all this by the following paragraph (abbreviated) from *The Little Flowers of St Francis*. The Latin manuscript from which this material was drawn was written about a hundred years after Francis's death, from accounts left by the first Friars:

> 'Francis was perplexed. Should he give himself wholly to prayer, or should he preach from time to time? So he said to one of the Friars, "Tell Sister Clare to pray, with some of her companions, that God will show me which way is best. And ask Brother Silvester to do the same" . . . The Friar returned. "Christ has given the same answer to both. You should go and preach throughout the world, because He chose you not for yourself alone, but to save others." Then said Francis, "Let us go, in the name of God." . . . He preached with such ardour that the men and women of the town were all eager to leave their homes and follow him. It was then that he decided on the Third Order.
>
> He saw some trees by the roadside on which rested an innumerable flock of birds. "Wait here," he said, "I will go and preach to my sisters the birds."
>
> "My little sisters, you have received many things from God, He preserved you in the Ark, that birds should not perish out of the world. You do not sow or reap, but He feeds you.
>
> You do not spin or sow, but you are clothed.
>
> Keep yourselves from the sin of ingratitude, and try always to please God." He made over them the sign of the Cross, and they rose in the air with a wonderful song . . . one flight going east, one west, one south, one north . . . So the preaching of the Cross, renewed by St Francis, would be borne by his friars through the whole world. And the friars, like the birds, would possess nothing for themselves, but trust the providence of God.' (*Little Flowers*, 15)

REBELS

It was difficult to decide on a title for this section of the chapter. In contrast to those who belonged to movements of spiritual renewal, a number of people were dissatisfied with the Church as it was, and tried to change it in an extreme way. They were therefore considered as heretics, at least by the Church leaders at that time. We shall see that the line dividing the 'spiritually renewed' from the 'heretical' movement is one which it is not easy to draw. Many Christians today find it difficult to agree with the judgement of the Church of the time.

THE POOR MEN OF LYONS (1176):
PETER WALDO (DIED 1217)

A vivid description of this society has been preserved. It was not made by a member of the society but by one who was examining the movement as a danger to the Church:

'A certain rich man of the city of Lyons (map, p. 32), called Waldo, was curious when he heard the Gospel read. He knew little Latin, but wanted to know what it said. So he made an arrangement with two priests, that one should translate it for him, and that the other should write it down. This they did. Waldo and his friends often read over the translations, and learned them by heart. Then Waldo proposed that he would take the Apostles' example as the pattern of the perfect life and try to follow it. He sold all his goods . . . and gave his money to the poor. Then he took upon himself the preaching of the Gospel, and those things that he had learned by heart, in the villages and open places. He called his hearers, men and women, to do the same, teaching them the Gospel by heart . . . And they, simple and uneducated men and women, wandered through villages, went into houses, preached in open places, and even in churches, and set still others going on the same course.' (*The Man of Laon*, sometimes called The Anonymous)

Here was a movement which arose suddenly and spread swiftly through the countryside. It extended up the valley of the river Rhone in eastern France, and across to the river Rhine and into the Netherlands and Germany. After the excitement of being in direct touch with the record of Jesus and His disciples, these simple folk concentrated upon the teaching which they found there. This led them to reject all the practices of the Church which they did *not* find there—confession to a priest and penance; prayers to saints and masses for the dead; images behind the altar; the taking of oaths ('Swear not at all,' Matt. 5.34); and the taking of life. As their leader was a layman, they continued to advocate lay preaching, and since they had parts of the Bible translated, they criticized the use of Latin in services. The Pope at first looked favourably upon their apostolic poverty, and allowed their lay preaching provided they had the bishop's consent.

Their numbers multiplied, and they spread to Italy. They had much in common with St Francis, except his intense devotion to the Church, e.g.

'Always obedient and submissive at the feet of holy Church' (*The Rule of St Francis*: Kidd, *Documents* III, pp. 158–161). Their development was towards separation from the Church, and in 1184 Pope and Council banned them as heretics. Persecuted by both Church and State, they survived in the high mountains of north Italy, and in Bohemia where they united with the Hussites (pp. 167, 168). They are represented today in Italy by the Waldensian Protestant Church of about twenty thousand members.

Some groups who were fighting against abuses in the Church, deserve to be called rebels much more than the Poor Men of Lyons. These were groups who came into conflict with the Pope. And there was one great bishop who, though not in conflict with the Pope, did criticize Pope Innocent IV.

ROBERT GROSSTESTE (1175–1253), BISHOP OF LINCOLN

Bishop Grosseteste was learned in a variety of subjects: the astronomy of his own period, the writings of the Fathers of the Early Church, and, further back, the pre-Christian philosophy of the Greeks. He was bishop of the largest bishopric in England, and was zealous in visiting every part of it, preaching, confirming, advising, and stirring people towards every sort of good work. That is how he believed the Church was to be lifted out of the evils of the time. And one evil of a different sort he faced boldly in his last few years.

Pope Innocent III had humbled John, king of England, by deposing him and making him kneel to receive back his crown. Since that time Popes had been responsible for a steady drain of money out of England. They claimed the right to make appointments to high positions in the English Church, and appointed Italians who would enjoy the income, without ever going to England, much less doing the work of the Church there. Grosseteste believed and taught that to make such appointments was to deprive souls of spiritual care, i.e. it was the worst form of simony. So when Pope Innocent IV named his own nephew for such an appointment in Lincoln, Grosseteste as bishop refused to receive him. This is how he wrote:

'It is impossible for the most holy Apostolic see (i.e. Rome) to command anything like this sin, which is so hateful to Jesus Christ. No faithful servant could submit to a command of this kind, even if it came from one of the highest angels. . . . As an obedient son, I disobey, I contradict, *I rebel*.'

Grosseteste was saying that God gave power to the Pope for the up-building of the Church. Anything which will destroy the Church does

John Wycliffe believed that the Bible should be available in the language of the people. Five of his friends translated the whole Bible into English, and he sent out preachers with written copies, who read it aloud to crowds in church or on the village green.
10.3   A fifteenth-century woodcut shows Wycliffe, Bible in hand.
10.4   The chair which Wycliffe used can still be seen at Lutterworth, the English parish where he worked.

not belong to that power, so the Pope cannot command it. Grossteste was not denying the Pope's authority, but pointing to the wrong use of it.

Grossteste was equally outspoken with the king, Henry III of England, and was father-in-God to Simon de Montfort, chief among the founders of the English parliament. His influence lasted on.

JOHN WYCLIFFE (1329-1384)

Wycliffe came from a village of that name near Barnard Castle in north Yorkshire. Educated at Oxford, he was Master of Balliol, a college with strong northern connections, in 1360. From about 1370 to 1382 he was the university's most able writer and teacher of philosophy and theology. He wrote much, but has left us little about himself or the university. For example, in 1355 the worst ever 'town and gown' riot broke out (p. 120). Townsmen attacked students with bows and arrows, burned colleges to the ground, and stopped all teaching, until the king intervened to defend the rights of students, but Wycliffe says nothing about it. He wrote much about Church and State, about what was wrong with both, and about how to put it right.

Wycliffe based his teaching on the idea of what he called 'dominion by grace'. 'Dominion', or 'lordship', means being a person with property or power. A king, prince, or noble had much property and great power, but an ordinary man had a few rights on local land, and had authority only in his own family. At that time, people thought that property and power could only be received from someone above them in feudal society. For example, a farmer could farm his land because he did service to his local lord; the lord served his prince; the prince served the king; and the king ruled by grace of God. Wycliffe disregarded the people in between, and taught that all property and all power comes from God. It is ours to use, so long as we use it rightly. If we misuse it, we should lose it. 'Rightly' means according to God's law, and God's law is to be found in the Bible. If we use rightly what God has given us, that is 'dominion by grace'.

This may seem a simple view of life and duty, not likely to raise problems. But the following are a few of the startling ideas which Wycliffe produced from his 'dominion by grace':

'The right to govern depends on right government.
There is no need to pay tax to bad rulers in Church or State.
Kings may take away possessions if the Church misuses them.
The Pope may be corrected, may even be accused, by his subjects.'

People listened to Wycliffe because he expressed some of their own discontents. Peasants listened, most of whom worked on other people's land. Later there rose from among them this revolutionary song, with the idea of a classless society:

'When Adam dug and Eve span,
Who was then the gentleman?'

In 1381 bands of peasants marched on London, and Wycliffe's enemies said that they had got their revolutionary ideas from him.

Merchants listened. They were complaining that every year the Pope took gold out of England, some said five times as much as the revenue of England's king. The Pope was a Frenchman, and England was at war with France.

Princes and nobles listened. In England the Church owned one-third of all the land. Wycliffe said that the Church should get rid of its wealth, and they agreed. Wycliffe was thinking of the poor, but the nobles were hoping to add Church lands to their own estates. One prince, the king's brother, John Duke of Lancaster, approved of Wycliffe's views so strongly that he took him under his protection.

People of all sorts and classes listened, and especially people who had a concern about religion. They agreed with Wycliffe when he said that religion in the Bible was different from religion as they saw it round about them. News of all this was carried to Rome. The Pope sent messages to the Archbishop of Canterbury and the Bishop of London. He told them to warn the king and nobles against Wycliffe, to arrest him, and have him sent to Rome for judgement before the Pope. But Wycliffe had powerful friends, and was the greatest figure in the university. So nothing was done till 1382, when the archbishop condemned his teaching. Wycliffe then retired from Oxford to his country church at Lutterworth, to continue his work from there for the remaining two years of his life.

WYCLIFFE AND THE CHURCH

Wycliffe's work was that of a reformer, opposing abuses, and so he was more often denying than affirming—saying what he did *not* believe rather than what he did believe. He seems to have become unnecessarily negative about the Church, especially as regards:
1. the Church in the New Testament,
2. the Church as the 'Elect',
3. Christ's presence in the Eucharist.

1. THE CHURCH IN THE NEW TESTAMENT

'Right', as we saw, for Wycliffe meant that which is according to God's law, i.e. the Bible. So his pattern for the Church was the Church of the New Testament. As students of Church history we know that the condition of the Church in New Testament times was that there was not a single church building, Christians were few, the world was heathen. Did Wycliffe mean that he ought to return to that? Or did he simply mean that we should return to New Testament faith about the Church? That would include faith that the Church should go on to 'greater works than these (works of Jesus)' (John 14.12); that its witness should reach 'governors and kings' (Mark 13.9); that it should fulfil its world mission (Luke 24.47).

2. THE CHURCH AS THE 'ELECT'

Wycliffe said that the true Church was the 'Elect'. By this word 'Elect' he meant those who had been predestined (chosen beforehand) by God to be saved. In contrast to the visible Church, this 'election' is invisible, known only to God. Wycliffe said that no man, not even the Pope himself, 'knows whether he is of the Church or whether he is a limb of the Devil'. This seems to leave little positive meaning for the Church here on earth.

3. CHRIST'S PRESENCE IN THE EUCHARIST

Wycliffe was outspoken about superstition on this subject. He believed in Christ's presence, but 'not materially nor bodily'. He said that he wanted 'to recall the Church from idolatry, because the purpose of the Sacrament was to make Christ present in the soul'.

Wycliffe most worthily represented his own faith when, after quoting the words of institution in the four New Testament passages, Matthew 26.26, Mark 14.22, Luke 22.19, and 1 Corinthians 11.23, he commented:

'All these agree, though the words differ slightly.
Christ, who could not lie, said that the bread which He took into His
    hand was His body . . .
This gives full confidence to the faithful.'

So Wycliffe would be able to join St Thomas Aquinas in his hymn for the Festival of Corpus Christi:

'Thy faithful word believing,
We take and doubt no more.' (See p. 117)

When we find Christ present in His Sacrament, a hymn is more profitable than an argument.

WYCLIFFE AND THE BIBLE

Wycliffe's positive and more permanent contribution to the Church concerned the Bible. When he spoke of 'right' use of that which is entrusted by God, he meant 'use according to God's law', as it is contained in the Bible. He looked beyond the Church to the Bible as the final authority for Christian teaching, and so he was concerned that all people should be able to understand the Bible. So he believed that the Bible should be available in the language of the people, and should be taught.

At this time in Europe great literature was being produced by men who stopped using Latin and wrote in German, French, Italian, Spanish, English; and parts of the Bible had already appeared in these languages. In English only parts of the Bible had yet been translated. Five of Wycliffe's Oxford friends translated the whole Bible from the Latin Vulgate into English.

And Wycliffe from Lutterworth sent out preachers, wearing long gowns of russet-coloured cloth, such as peasants' clothes were made of, with a staff in their hand, and without purse. There was as yet no printing press, so these preachers went with written copies, and read aloud to crowds who gathered in the church, or round the market cross, or on the village green. Some passages they taught the people to repeat after them over and over again, so that even if they could not put the Bible into their hands, they could leave them with some of its words in their hearts: 'Our Father', the Ten Commandments, a Psalm, the Sermon on the Mount. And often they preached about what the Bible says.

In 1408 the Archbishop of Canterbury condemned this translation, and forbade any further translation, or the use of one, without a Bishop's licence. But the seed had been sown. There were people now who knew what it was like to have the Bible in their own language, and to oppose this burst of new life would soon prove to be like trying to stop the coming of the tide, or of the spring, or the monsoon season.

STUDY SUGGESTIONS

WORD STUDY

1. What is the origin of the following words and phrases?
   (a) Abbot (b) chapter house (c) Cistercian (d) *Opus Dei*

REVIEW OF CONTENT

2. (a) What led Benedict to withdraw from the world?
   (b) Where and when did he build his monastery?
3. (a) What was Benedict's ideal for his monks?
   (b) On whose earlier Rule was the Rule of St Benedict partly based?
   (c) What were the two chief emphases in Benedict's Rule?
   (d) How did Benedict divide up the hours of the day for his monks?
   (e) What was the 'Work of God'?

4. What problems made it difficult for many monasteries to achieve and maintain the ideal progress under the Rule as laid down by Benedict himself?

5. When, how, and by whom was the Benedictine monastery at Cluny founded?

6. (a) In what ways did the Cluniacs change and develop some of the rules laid down by Benedict?
(b) Which particular characteristics of the monastery at Cluny encouraged the establishment of other Cluniac monasteries?

7. (a) How did the Cistercian Order begin?
(b) What was the special aim of the Cistercians?
(c) Why were they called 'white' monks?

8. (a) Who was the most famous Cistercian, and when did he live?
(b) Why did 'mothers hide from him their sons, wives their husbands, men their friends'?

9. (a) What was 'the most important movement of spiritual renewal in the later Middle Ages'?
(b) Why was it so important?

10. (a) Who were the Albigenses?
(b) What were their leaders called?
(c) What ideas did they combine with Christian teaching?
(d) Who was sent as a missionary to them?

11. Describe again some of the things which the Franciscan and Dominican Orders had in common, and some in which they differed.

12. (a) In what circumstances did Francis decide to establish the Third Order of Franciscans?
(b) Describe in your own words Francis's preaching to the birds.

13. (a) What sort of movement did Peter Waldo start?
(b) How did its members live?
(c) What attitude towards them did the Pope take?
(d) In which Church is the remnant of them to be found today?

14. (a) What great bishop in England criticized Pope Innocent IV?
(b) For what did he criticize him?
(c) Did he criticize *only* the Pope?

15. (a) When did John Wycliffe live?
(b) What did he chiefly write about?
(c) Who were the people who chiefly listened to Wycliffe, and why?
(d) What was the Pope's reaction to Wycliffe's teaching?

16. (a) What was Wycliffe's most positive and permanent contribution to the Church?
(b) Describe how his followers took the Bible to the people of England?
(c) Who is carrying on this work today?

DISCUSSION AND RESEARCH

17. Wycliffe 'looked beyond the Church to the Bible as the final authority for Christian teaching'.
Did the Church authorities of his day think that he was right to do so? What is your own opinion?

18. 'A number of people were dissatisfied with the Church and tried to change it in an extreme way.' (p. 151)
Do you think it is best to show one's disapproval of the Church by leaving it, or by trying to change it from the inside? Give your reasons.

19. 'Monasticism began as a movement of spiritual renewal.' (p. 143)
What other movements of spiritual renewal do you know of in the history of the Church, and how successful have they been?

20. Which, if any, of the Day or Night Hours in Benedict's scheme of worship are observed in your Church or in any Church that you know? Are they observed every day? What is the chief benefit of this sort of regular worship? What, if any, are its dangers?

21. (a) List some of those who tried in the Middle Ages to renew the Church by changing its structure and activities, rather than its spiritual life.
(b) List some of those who do this today. How successful do you think they are likely to be?

22. On what principle did Wycliffe base his teaching and what sort of ideas did he base on it? What is your opinion of his teaching?

23. 'Wycliffe said that the true Church was the "Elect"—meaning that some people are predestined by God to be saved.'
Do you agree with the statement (p. 157) that 'this seems to leave little positive meaning for the Church here on earth'? Give reasons for your answer.

24. Find out all you can about the movements of 'renewal' in the Church which were led by the following men, and compare their results with those of the movements described in this chapter.
John Henry Newman   Billy Graham
George Fox   Frank Buchman

CHAPTER 11

More Setbacks:
West and East

The title of this book was suggested by Professor K. S. Latourette's seven volumes, *History of the Expansion of Christianity*. His is the biggest work in Church history done by anybody in this century, and the widest in scope that anyone has ever done. Professor Latourette sees the rise and fall in the Church's fortunes as shown in the chart and graph below. This is his summary of conclusions:

'It seems clear that the influence of Jesus has been rising, that each peak, in its effects, has been higher than the previous peak, and that each recess has, on the whole, been marked by a smaller loss than its predecessor . . . Each advance has set a new mark for the influence of Jesus in the total life of mankind.' (From two smaller books, *Anno Domini*, p. 219, and *The Unquenchable Light*, p. 171)

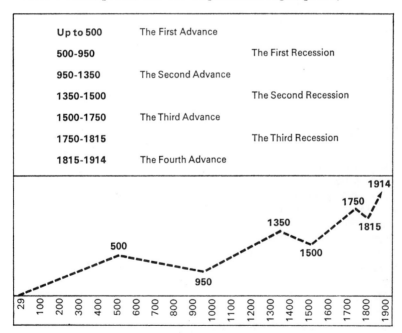

Up to 500	The First Advance	
500-950		The First Recession
950-1350	The Second Advance	
1350-1500		The Second Recession
1500-1750	The Third Advance	
1750-1815		The Third Recession
1815-1914	The Fourth Advance	

Chart 4: Peaks and recessions in the history of Church growth

161

At this point in our study, i.e. the beginning of the fourteenth century AD, we have arrived at the Second Recession, or to use the word which we have chosen, the Second Setback. We shall probably understand it best if we remember the First Recession, described in chapters 1 and 2, and look again at Setback in the West and then Setback in the East. We shall then end this book happily with the prospects of a new age, before going on to the next volume.

SETBACK IN THE WEST

At the end of Chapter 10 we saw what a muddle the situation in the Church of the West had become. In trying to bring about the Kingdom of God on earth, with the Pope as Vicar of Christ, the Papacy had become a power among the nations. In some periods it held supreme political power, representing the Church as above the nations of the world.

Then Pope Boniface VIII had rebuked the king of France for taxing the clergy. The king of France had answered back, saying that he had 'the advice of Parliament' on his side. He felt confident in his strong nation and state, which could no longer be easily divided and defeated as it had been in feudal times. The Pope was similarly rebuffed by the English Parliament which protested directly to him against his interfering in King Edward I's affairs. But the French king went further. He acted violently against the aging Pope, and brought him to his death in 1303. The next Pope issued a Bull (i.e. a written order) rightly condemning this violence. But he lived only four weeks more.

THE AVIGNON PAPACY (1305–1378)

No successor was appointed for nearly a year, and then the new Pope chosen was not an Italian as was usual, but a Frenchman, Clement V. He announced twelve new Cardinals, who were all French, except for one Englishman as a slight concession to France's enemy.

Clement also moved the seat of the Papacy from Rome to Avignon in Provence, a small independent state which was already dominated, and soon absorbed, by France. The Avignon Papacy lasted for seventy years, spoken of as 'the Babylonian captivity of the Church' (see Jer. 25.11) by critics who saw that the Papacy was declining in power. There were many critics, who disapproved not only of the move from Rome into France, but also of the fact that seven Frenchmen in succession were chosen as Pope.

For England the Hundred Years War with France began, and the anti-papal feeling of the thirteenth century was heightened when for seventy years the Papacy was dominated by England's foes.

11.1 'Outspoken criticism of the Pope was widespread'. (p. 164)
St Catherine of Siena complained of the Pope's desertion of Rome, and told Gregory
IX that he should win back souls rather than the Papacy's earthly possessions.
Francesco Vanni's painting in the church of St Dominic in Siena is believed to be
an authentic portrait of her.

163

Even for the French, the Avignon Papacy was not all gain. In moving from Rome the Pope had to leave lands and properties and sources of income behind. The change-over did bring opportunity for reform of some abuses in the Church's administration, and this good must be acknowledged. But the move to Avignon meant vast new expenses, which had to be met by levies on the Churches, and the Churches nearest at hand were those of France.

Outspoken criticism of the Pope was widespread, often from surprising people. The most remarkable female figure in later medieval Church history is St Catherine of Siena. As an Italian, she could be expected to complain of the Pope's desertion of Rome. But she was, more than an Italian, a saint, and was deeply devoted to the Church and to the Pope himself. These were her words to Pope Gregory XI:

'If you would open the eyes of your intelligence, you would see, Holy Father, that it is more necessary for you to win back souls than to recover your earthly possessions.'

As a Dominican said on a similar occasion, 'I was astonished with what authority words like these were spoken in the presence of so great a pontiff.'

A return to Rome was contemplated by Pope Urban V (1362–1370), the seventh Avignon Pope. He went to Rome. Streets were quiet. Great houses were shuttered and empty. Many buildings, including historic churches, were in need of repair. He felt that it would be hard to leave the luxurious courts of Avignon for this.

Gregory XI (1370) did make the break. He moved back to Rome in 1377, but died during the following year.

The cardinals were divided. They were nearly all Frenchmen, and in their hearts wanted the Papacy to remain in Avignon. But the election of a new Pope must now be held in Rome. In Rome there was always the mob, and the mob was shouting, 'A Roman! A Roman!' The Pope elected was not a Roman, but they did call a man from Naples, to be Pope Urban VI. He was strict, of high ideals, but lacked tact and patience. He would have no talk of going back to Avignon, and soon he had many enemies. His cardinals discussed how to correct their mistake in choosing him, and decided that an election made under pressure from a mob could be declared invalid.

The French majority now elected one of their own number as Pope Clement VII. He was a soldier, related to the king of France, and he moved to Avignon. Urban VI said that the whole action was illegal, refused to recognize that Clement VII existed, and appointed new cardinals in place of those who had deserted him. So began the Schism.

THE SCHISM (1378-1417)

'Schism' means 'a tearing', and it was a tearing in two of the Church of the West. There were now two men claiming to be Pope, one Italian in Rome, the other French in Avignon. And there were two groups of cardinals; in one the majority were Italians, in the other, Frenchmen. And the various parts of the Church began to choose which they would recognize.

The Pope in Rome was recognized, obviously, by Italy; by England since she was at war with France; by most of Germany, whose rulers were mistrustful of the French; and also by Scandinavia and Portugal.

The Pope in Avignon was recognized by France, inevitably; by Scotland, because England had gone the other way; and by the rest of Germany. Notice that the choice was made because of *national* interests. The ideal of a Church that would be *above* national interests was made a mockery. Here was a scandal indeed, and how could it be ended? Neither Pope would resign. Both could claim canonical election, i.e. election according to the rules, by duly appointed cardinals. The question was put to the university of Paris, and, from some of the wisest there, came the answer, 'By a Council'. Two of the most learned who gave this answer were Pierre (Peter) d'Ailly (1350-1420), and Jean (John) de Gerson (1363-1429).

RULE BY COUNCIL

D'Ailly was Chancellor of Paris University in 1389, and later Bishop of Cambrai. The chief concern of his life was the healing of this Schism. He was learned in many subjects, and wrote a book called *The Likeness of the Universe*, putting forward the theory that men might reach India, which was at that time cut off from Europe by the Ottoman Turks (p. 171), by sailing westward. This book is said to have been used by Columbus (p. 185). Gerson was one of his students, who succeeded him as Chancellor in 1395. The two were lifelong friends, and what they did in this period's controversies influenced what came to be known as 'Gallicanism' (Gallic means belonging to 'Gaul', the old Roman name for France). This was a view held by many Church leaders, who claimed that more freedom should be allowed for *national* expression within the Church in France.

D'Ailly and Gerson both believed that the 'full power' of the Church lay, not in the Pope its head, but in the whole body, and that this body could be represented only in a Council of representatives from the whole Church. The civil power (e.g. the Emperor) could summon the Council, since the first Council, held at Nicaea in 325 (see Vol. 1, p. 139), was summoned by Constantine. Christ also 'was obedient to' His Mother

(Luke 2.51), which the Vicar of Christ might take as example in relation to Mother Church. However, having little faith that either Pope would obey the ruling of such a Council, these distinguished university men persuaded the king of France to withdraw his recognition of the Avignon Pope, and then brought the two rival groups of cardinals together. It was found that both France and England would support the calling of a Council, and that other nations were sure to follow. The Council opened in 1409.

1. THE COUNCIL OF PISA (1409)

Most of the cardinals saw the need to end the Schism, which was ruinous to the prestige of Cardinals as well as Pope, and indeed ruinous to the prestige of the whole Church. The Council declared both Popes deposed, and elected a successor, Alexander V. It is almost unbelievable that no one had considered what should be done to make the deposed Popes resign, and both of them refused. So, with the new Pope added, there were now three. The scandal of the Schism was increased. So a second Council was called, which met at Constance (see map 3B, p. 32).

2. THE COUNCIL OF CONSTANCE
(1414–1418)

This Council was a much more imposing affair than the one at Pisa. One of the three Popes was persuaded by the Emperor to summon the Council. He did so hoping that he might be the one not to be deposed, but later abdicated. Princes were bidden to attend as well as arch-bishops, bishops, abbots, and heads of orders, and the Holy Roman Emperor presided. It was an assembly worthy of discussing the whole international situation. The remaining two Popes were deposed, and the Council declared itself the Church's supreme authority (Kidd, *Documents* III, p. 209). Some difficult subjects were dealt with, but instead of going through the whole list of desired reforms, it was decreed that regular councils should be held, every ten years. A new Pope was elected, and thus the Schism was healed.

The new Pope was Martin V. Alas! He was a Pope of the old sort, and denied that a Council of the Church had an authority beyond that of the Pope:

'No one may appeal from the supreme judge, the Vicar of Christ, or may decline His authority in matters of faith.'

Gerson declared that this statement, if accepted by the Council, would make nonsense of all that the Council had decided, including Martin V's own election as Pope. But the Council had begun on 1 November, 1414, and it was now November, 1417, time to go home.

Anyone experienced in diplomacy should have known that, if the work of reform was to be completed, it must *precede* the election of a Pope. Once elected, he would inevitably block decisions by the Council. Gerson and his party were used to administration in a university, where students were divided into 'nations', which were actually larger groupings including several nationalities. In the Council of Constance too, voting had been by national groups, but each nation voted separately and their interests were often opposed.

Martin V was enough of a diplomatist to offer to one nation a concession, to another an exemption, to a third, a measure of reform. He might have taken as his motto 'Divide and rule'. And even though some problems might be left unsolved, everyone wanted to get home.

But, sadly, one problem which *had* been settled at Constance was the case of John Huss.

JOHN HUSS (1373–1415)

The kingdom of Bohemia was a Slav state within the Holy Roman Empire. Today it is called Czechoslovakia. A reform movement, similar to that of Wycliffe, began there, marked by a return to emphasis on the Bible:

'Instead of carrying with me the supposed bone of a saint, I decided to make the Bible my companion on life's pilgrimage.' (Matthias of Jarrow)

Bohemia was also at that time undergoing a revival of national spirit. Huss became the leader, and under him these two movements flowed together: reformed religion and Czech nationalism.

John Huss had been made a priest in 1402. Educated in the new university of Prague, he became Professor of Philosophy, and later Chancellor. He became a great preacher and preferred to preach in the Czech language, not for patriotic reasons, but in order to reach the mass of the people. He preached the Headship of Christ, not of St Peter. His motive was not so much to attack the Pope, as to return to New Testament moral standards (Kidd, *Documents* III, p. 213).

Huss's movement was helped by events in England, where King Richard II took Anne of Bohemia, the king's sister, as his queen. Much coming and going between Oxford and Prague universities resulted. The latter had grown to be the biggest and most distinguished in all the Holy Roman Empire. From Oxford, Czech students brought back much intellectual support for reform in their own Church. In Prague University strong rivalry arose between German conservatives and Czech reformers, i.e. Hussites. In 1409 the Czech-Hussite party triumphed, and the non-Slav staff and students withdrew and founded the (German) university of Leipzig.

In 1410 this division was recognized as a problem which was more than local (Prague's), national (the Czechs'), or even imperial. It threatened the unity of the whole Church of the West. On demand of the Pope and the Archbishop of Prague, Wycliffe's books were burned in the square at Prague, and Huss was declared excommunicated. Huss was summoned to appear before the Council of Constance, and the Emperor encouraged him to go, promising to protect him. Huss went expecting theological debate, but instead he was tried as a heretic, and the Emperor was powerless to help him. Huss was already excommunicated, and so was beyond the Emperor's protection. Besides, the Church of the West had turned to Councils, because of a problem (the Schism) which was beyond the power of the Pope. So no chance must be given for the Pope to interfere on the grounds that there was a problem which the Council could not settle. Even good men of enlightened views, such as d'Ailly and Gerson, agreed that the Council must be shown to be the supreme authority in the Church, or its purpose would fail. So the Council condemned Huss, and he was burned.

The third Council was that of Basle.

3. THE COUNCIL OF BASLE (1431–1449)

Pope Martin died in 1431, and before electing his successor, the cardinals drew up demands which he would have to accept: to respect the rights of the cardinals, to give them control of half the Church's revenues, to reform the Church's administration, and to call a Council. The Pope was Eugenius IV; the Council met in 1431.

This time it did not vote by nations. Instead, it divided into commissions—one for the Hussite problem; one on reunion with the Greek Church; one on reforms. In the first there was some success, concessions were made to more moderate Hussites, which brought a chance of peace. The second, alas, had no success. Reunion with the Greeks was too much to hope for, unless they were assured of a Crusade to save them from the Ottoman Turks (p. 171, below). And reforms were few compared with the hopes with which the Council opened.

The Council took years to die, but it did die, and that was the end of the attempts to unite the Church by this means. D'Ailly and Gerson, its leaders, were far-sighted men, who aspired towards a Church ruled by its Council, within which the new factor of *nation*hood might be represented and expressed. But hopes that a Council might save the Church from all its troubles faded. Perhaps the idea had come too soon, and people's hopes had soared too high and too far ahead of the times.

11.2 'John Huss preached the Headship of Christ, not of St Peter.' He was summoned to appear before the Council of Constance, and was tried as a heretic. The Council condemned Huss, and in 1415 he was burned at the stake.
This seventeenth-century print depicts his martyrdom.

11.3 In the early fourteenth century Franciscan Friars recruited for the 'breathtaking opportunity' for mission to the Mongol Khan. But the facts are that the mission was far too late and too small. In the massacres caused by Tamerlane, many Christians of the Church of the East were martyred, as shown in Lorenzetto's painting in the church of St Francis at Siena.

After all, in political affairs there was as yet no 'constitutional' monarch in Europe (i.e. a king ruling according to laws decided by his Parliament). So it was probably unrealistic to hope for a 'constitutional' Papacy. The leaders of this period had not yet found even the words with which to express the idea.

RODRIGO BORGIA (1493)

The end of the fifteenth century brought an end to hopes of every kind. In 1493 Rodrigo Borgia became Pope Alexander VI, a man who was both irreligious and immoral, whom it would be blasphemy to speak of as Vicar of Christ. How did this happen?

It was as if five hundred years had gone for nothing; as if men like Nicholas II and Leo IX, Hildebrand and Innocent III had never lived. As if there had been no lofty ideals:

'Even now is the Church the Kingdom of Christ, and His saints now reign with Him.'

or:

'The Pope as the Head of Christendom—
The Pope as the Vicar of Christ.'

Rome was again just the centre of a small Italian princedom, ruled by a worldling prince, and once again needed to be cleansed.

But this time who would undertake the cleansing?

SETBACK IN THE EAST

In Chapter 2 we saw that the rise of Islam and the Arab invasions threatened the very existence of Christendom by an encircling movement (map, p. 17). This was broken, first by the Byzantine Emperor Leo's defence of his capital, Constantinople, in 718, and then by Charles Martel's victory at Tours in France in 732. The Arabs overran half the territory which had been the Christian Roman Empire, including the land of Christianity's origin, Palestine, and the lands of its early strength, Syria, Asia Minor, Egypt, North Africa. These lands became Muslim-ruled. In some there was a continuing, but shrinking, Christian minority. In North Africa no Christianity survived at all.

In the second period of setback Eastern Europe was added to this tragic list, following the fall of Constantinople in 1453. But there had in the meantime been a loss to Islam in eastern and central Asia. This was an area, not of Christianity's early strength, but of recent opportunity.

In chapter 6 we saw the breath-taking opportunity for missions to the Mongol Khans. As nomads, content to remain simple animists, they had come to rule almost the whole of Asia, except India, and were ready to choose one of the three great religions, Islam in the west, Buddhism in the east, or Christianity scattered over the whole. For a quarter of a century, 1269–1294, there was a chance that they might choose Christianity. Here is Marco Polo's opinion, which we did not quote before:

> 'If men should have been sent by the Pope suited to preach our Faith to him, the Great Khan would have been made a Christian, because it is known for certain that he had a great desire to be so.'

Kublai himself in his message to the Pope had foretold 'more Christians here than in your parts'. If it had happened, Christianity would have been reinvigorated by this mission-of-help, and might have spread from Mongols and other non-Chinese peoples to the Chinese themselves (see p. 80) and so have survived in China. It might even have spread to the Mongols of central Asia, before Babar led them over the Himalayas in 1526 to found a kingdom in Hindustan, and permanently plant their religion there. The history of all Asia might have been different.

But these are might-have-beens. The facts of history are that by 1300 the Mongols were turning, not to Christianity, but in the east to Buddhism, and in central and western Asia to Islam. In 1368 China expelled her Mongol rulers, and set up a Chinese dynasty again, the Ming dynasty. Non-Chinese communities, brought in by foreign rule, were in disfavour, and moved westward. So, for the second time, Christianity disappeared from Chinese territory.

In central Asia a fanatical Muslim of Mongol race came to power at this time. He was called Timur in Chinese, Tamerlane in English (1336–1405). His tomb of beautiful enamelled bricks at Samarkand is the only thing left associated with him which is not horrible. He set out to copy the exploits of Genghis Khan. Unlike Genghis (p. 79), he did not start from the hard life of a nomad tribe, but from a luxurious court where his body now lies. His armies ravaged westward to the river Volga, south to India, east to China, leaving destruction everywhere. The massacres which he caused reduced the populations of central Asia, which did not recover till modern times. By the time of his death the Onguts, Keraits, Uighurs, and other tribes among whom were many Christians, had disappeared. Those who escaped massacre were absorbed into Islam. Christians of the Church of the East, who had lived in China or on its frontiers for eight hundred years, had ceased to be.

The most devastating loss of Christian territory to Islam came with the rise to power of a small Turkish tribe, the Ottomans, on the eastern frontiers of the Byzantine Empire in Asia Minor. Here they founded a Muslim state, with an army which was almost invincible. Its core was composed of slaves, forcibly taken as children from Christian homes, brought up apart from all tender influences, and turned into fighting men and nothing more. In 1356 the Ottoman Turks crossed to Europe, and by the end of the century they had subdued all of the Balkans. Constantinople remained as the Christian capital of an empire, which, as a result of this invasion, came to its end.

Constantinople too would have fallen, but for Tamerlane. This destroyer of central Asia happened at this very time to reach over into Asia Minor, to destroy with his Mongol horsemen an Ottoman army and most of the Ottoman state.

It took 50 years for the Turks to recover, but in 1453 their state had been remade, and their army was ready to finish its task. Constantinople fell. By a grim irony, the last Roman Emperor, who died in the street fighting, bore the name Constantine, like the city's founder. This was Constantine XI. And the Sultan of the victorious Turks was Muhammad II.

Between 638 and 640 Jerusalem, Antioch, and Alexandria, all Great Sees, had fallen before the Arab invasion. For eight hundred years, apart from Rome in the west, only Constantinople out of all the Patriarchates of the early Church had remained free from Muslim rule. Roman civilization in the west had been overrun by northern barbarians in the fifth century, so for a thousand years Constantinople had stood for the continuing life of the Christian Roman Empire. Now all this was gone. The Christian populations of south-east Europe came under an oppressive Muslim rule, which for some was broken only at the end of the first World War in 1918. Constantine's Christian capital was renamed Istanbul.

This volume, *Setback and Recovery*, began with that crowning glory of early Christian architecture, the church of the Holy Wisdom in Constantinople. In 1453 it had become a Muslim mosque.

STUDY SUGGESTIONS

WORD STUDY

1. What is the origin of the word 'Gallicanism' and what does it mean?
2. What does the word 'Schism' mean, and for what event in the history of the Church is it used, according to this chapter? For what other events is it sometimes used.

REVIEW OF CONTENT

3. Give approximate dates for:
   (a) Each of the four chief periods of advance in the Church's history.

(b) Each of the three chief periods of setback in the Church's history.
4. (a) Which two kings stood in opposition to Pope Boniface VIII?
(b) Which of these kings seemed to have gained by the appointment of the next Pope but one, Clement V?
5. (a) What two things in particular did Pope Clement V do which aroused criticism in the Church?
(b) For what did Catherine of Siena chiefly criticize the Pope?
6. (a) How long did the Avignon papacy last?
(b) In what ways did the Church in France lose, instead of gaining, as a result of the Avignon papacy?
7. (a) Which Pope first tried to move the papacy back to Rome?
(b) Which Pope actually did move back to Rome, and when?
(c) Why were the French cardinals afraid of holding the papal election in Rome?
8. Explain how the papal election in 1377 led to what was called the Schism?
9. Which countries recognized the Pope in Rome, and which recognized the Pope in Avignon, and for what reasons?
10. Who were the two learned men who suggested how the Schism might be healed, and what did they suggest?
11. What were the dates of the Councils of Pisa, Constance, and Basle, and who was responsible for calling each of them?
12. (a) What was the chief result of the Council of Pisa?
(b) What was the chief result of the Council of Constance?
13. Why was the work of reform approved at the Council of Constance eventually held up?
14. (a) Who was John Huss and when did he live?
(b) What was his chief work?
(c) Why was he excommunicated?
(d) Why was the emperor unable to protect him at the Council of Constance?
15. In what ways did the organization of the Council of Basle differ from that of the Councils of Pisa and Constance?
16. What 'territory' had been lost to Christianity by the end of the fifteenth century as a result of Arab invasions?
17. Who was Tamerlane?
18. (a) What Muslim tribe caused the worst loss of Christian territory?
(b) What sort of army did they have?
(c) Why did Constantinople not fall to this tribe when they crossed from Asia into Europe in 1356?
19. (a) When did Constantinople eventually fall to Islam?
(b) Who was the last Roman emperor to rule in Constantinople?
(c) What new name did the Muslims give to Constantinople?

DISCUSSION AND RESEARCH

20. (a) To what present-day country does the city which used to be called Constantinople belong?

(b) What is the attitude of that country's rulers towards Christians?

21. (a) What different sorts of 'schism' exist in the Church today?

(b) What means, if any, does the Church use for healing them, and to what extent are these means successful?

22. (a) Explain the statement (p. 170) that 'it was as if 500 years had gone for nothing: as if men like Nicholas II and Leo IX, Hildebrand and Innocent III had never lived'.

(b) Do you think it is ever true to say that the work of great Christians has 'gone for nothing'?

23. The massacres which Tamerlane caused reduced the population of Central Asia.

What modern ruler or rulers had a similar effect on the populations of eastern Europe?

CHAPTER 12

Prospects of a New Age:
New Learning and New World

In working through this book we have made a long journey; a thousand years long in time; and in space, going here and there across three continents. Perhaps it seems to be a journey leading nowhere. So let us look back over the way along which we have come.

REVIEW, AD 500–1500

We began with a Setback in the West about 500; the fall of the Roman Empire. That had been the civilization whose Roman peace and communications, and whose Greek language, gave to the Christian religion the right conditions for its first advance (chapter 1). Then came a Setback in the East, 622, the rise of Islam (chapter 2).

Next we considered 'another more northerly advance'. That was the conversion to Christianity of the Anglo-Saxons (597), and, mostly through them, the conversion of all northern Europe (690–c. 1000) (chapter 3).

To the east of Latin and Greek-speaking Christians, we saw how Persian monks, with their Bible and liturgy in Syriac, in 635 completed Christianity's eastward progress, and reached the capital of China (chapter 4).

Among the Franks we saw the civilized Charlemagne crowned Emperor in 800; and a little later, among Slavs of Moravia, we saw Greek missionaries translate the Bible into the Slavonic language for 'future benefit of all the Slavs, and Russia' (chapter 5).

The thirteenth century brought breath-taking missionary opportunity among the Mongols, and in 1281 a monk from China became *Catholicos* (Patriarch) of the Church of the East (chapter 6).

Coming back to the Church of the West we looked at Church life, the clergy and their training, and three centuries of great church building (1050–1350) (chapter 7). In two of those centuries (1050–1250) there were great Christian scholars (Schoolmen) and the beginning of universities (chapter 8).

We saw that throughout the medieval period the central figure in the Church of the West was the Pope, and we watched the varying success of efforts to make real his headship of Christendom (858–1305) (chapter 9).

We found new spiritual life, mostly in the West, coming to expression in various monastic movements, and in the Friars (chapter 10).

Then came setback again, in both West and East (chapter 11). These setbacks seem to bring to nothing the so many and varied achievements of the Church of the Middle Ages. Did what we called our 'long journey' in fact lead nowhere? It may well seem to, for by the year 1500:

1. The Syriac Church of the East had disappeared in east Asia and throughout central Asia. One small tribe remained Christian in Mesopotamia, with a much larger remnant, which is today called the Syrian Orthodox Church, in India, especially in the south.

2. The Greek Church had survived, and was capable of spreading as Russian rule spread eastward. But elsewhere it was shattered by the assaults of Muslim invaders, and was shut in, a shadow of its former self.

3. The Church of the West, with the Pope as guardian of its unity, had seen the Papacy become a subject for division and a declining spiritual power.

Such was the Church's condition about the year 1500. The most dramatic closing of the door upon the past was the fall of Constantinople to the Ottoman Turks in 1453. The last remnant of the Roman Empire was gone, dead and done with.

But there is another side to the history of the fifteenth century. Historians call it the century of the Renaissance. That does not mean 'dead and done with', but *rebirth*.

THE RENAISSANCE,
THE REVIVAL OF LEARNING,
THE NEW LEARNING

All these names were used for this exciting happening. The people of western Europe rediscovered the glories of ancient Greco-Roman civilization. This rediscovery stimulated, first in Italy, and then more widely, a burst of new painting, sculpture, architecture, and writing. Scholars became interested in the study of history, historical and literary criticism; and in scientific investigation and invention. The invention of the printing press made it possible for many more people to enjoy learning. Seamen competed with one another in voyages of exploration. At no other time in the Middle Ages was there such a spring of new life. We cannot in this book study the movement as a whole, so it seems best to choose one man to illustrate the movement: Pope Nicholas V (1447–1455). We have chosen him partly because in 1451 he issued a Bull (order) to establish a university at Glasgow in Scotland where the author of this book was Professor for twenty years. But, as you will see, there are other good reasons for our choice.

Nicholas V was the first, and best, of the Renaissance Popes. He was Pope when Constantinople fell (1453), and he was so distressed about it, and about the failure of his effort to rouse the princes and kings of Christendom to a Crusade to save it, that his distress shortened his life. He was scholarly, artistic, interested in science. He restored several ancient churches in Rome and had plans to rebuild the Vatican (the Pope's residence and the Church's headquarters), and the great church of St Peter, which stand together on Vatican Hill. Both these schemes had to wait, but Pope Nicholas did found the great Vatican Library.

A scholar named Valla proved at about this time that the *Donation of Constantine* (see p. 128), which for seven hundred years had been regarded as the authority for many powers claimed by the Popes, was nothing but make-believe. Instead of objecting, Pope Nicholas recognized Valla's work as capable critical study, and appointed him as his secretary. The Pope hoped to bring the Church into harmony with the Renaissance, and perhaps encourage it to take the lead in this new learning. He was thrilled by the exploration which Portugal's seamen had begun (see p. 180).

Many aspects of the Renaissance were big with promise for the Church. Two of them were especially important: (1) the printing press, and (2) the voyages of discovery.

THE PRINTING PRESS

As we saw, the Renaissance was a time of many new inventions. The most important of these for the Church, and indeed for mankind, was the printing press. Printing reached Italy too late for Pope Nicholas. It was most prominent in Germany's Renaissance.

The Chinese had a recipe for making cheap paper, and the Arabs had learned it from them, and introduced it to the west twelve hundred years ago—but not yet printing. The Chinese printed on their paper by using wooden blocks. Chinese is a language of monosyllables, but one syllable sometimes requires more than thirty strokes of the brush-pen to write it. Having written the elaborate letter, or 'character', they would stamp it upon the block while the ink was wet, and later carve round the letter's 'negative' (i.e. its shape in reverse), and then use the block to print from.

Printing like this, the Chinese were centuries ahead of any other country. Printing reached the west at this period of Renaissance, and was not only learned but immediately improved upon. John Gutenberg of Mainz in Germany (map 3B) began to use *movable type* for printing about the year 1450. Printing spread like wildfire. Printing presses reached Italy by 1465, and were being used in Paris in 1470, London in 1477, Stockholm in 1483, Madrid in 1499.

12.1 The Renaissance was a time of many new inventions. The most important of these for the Church was the printing press. Books had previously been few but now they became 'the heralds of the Gospel and the preachers of truth and science'. (p. 179)

A woodcut of 1511 shows the sort of press used for early printed editions of the Bible and other religious books.

Printing presses spread so quickly because many of the German printers were not just businessmen working to make money. They were enthusiastic craftsmen, giving themselves to what Europe at this time called 'the German art'. One German bishop called it 'a divine art'. All who cared for education recognized it as a step forward for mankind. Perhaps when we come across unwholesome books, magazines, or newspapers, we may hesitate to share their judgement that the press was a step forward. However, to judge otherwise is like wishing that man had not made the wheel because there are so many road accidents. In accepting an invention, we have to accept also that it may be misused. This is how a German educationist of the time described the 'missionary' spirit of German printers:

'As the Apostles went through the world with the good news, so in our days the disciples of the new art (printing) spread themselves through all countries, and their books are the heralds of the Gospel and the preachers of truth and science.' (Jacob Wimpfeling)

It is no wonder that he used the New Testament as illustration of what was happening. At the beginning, most of the books printed were religious books. In the first fifty years of German printing there were more than a hundred editions of the Bible, which was the book in most demand. The clergy were still the best educated people, and all education was in the hands of the Church.

With regard to the general step forward for mankind, this is the measure of the change. Books had previously been few, because they had to be copied by hand. Hardly anybody had many books of his own, because, being hand-copied, they were so expensive. Most people had not even one—so why bother to learn to read? But soon books were to become many and cheap; not yet books for all, but books for the many.

So the next step was to put books into the language of the many, not just Latin for the learned few, and to teach more and more people to read. This was to be the spirit of the new age. Those who were concerned, not about books in general but about the Scriptures in particular, may be represented by Erasmus of Rotterdam, all Europe's greatest scholar:

'I wish that they (the scriptures) might be translated into all the languages of Christian people, that they might be read and known, not merely by the Scots and the Irish, but by the Turks and Muslims. I wish that the farmer might sing parts of them at the plough, that the weaver may hum them at his shuttle, that the traveller may with their stories make the journey seem not so long.' (Erasmus, *Works* I, 142, 202 ff.)

In the age beyond 1500, which is our modern age, the Bible came into its own. *Ta Biblia* (Greek) literally means 'the books'. They were to be *the* books in a world which throughout the modern age has been heading towards literacy, an age in which the Bible has come to be available at last in almost all the world's languages. In a large number of languages the Bible was the first book in a new literature, as it was for the Teutonic (i.e. German) peoples of north Europe, including the English, and for some languages of central Asia (see Vol. 1, pp. 122 and 126). To these, the Slavonic languages, including Russian, had already been added (pp. 64, 65).

THE VOYAGES OF DISCOVERY

Pope Nicholas V did express his interest in exploration. In first mentioning him we noted his concern for Constantinople, and the failure of his own attempts to rouse Western Christendom to a crusade:

> 'The Vicar of Christ looks with fatherly care on all the world, and the nations in it, desiring the salvation of all . . . This will be helped if we give our favour to those kings and princes who, as champions of the Christian Faith, have put down fierce Muslims and other unbelievers.' (Nicholas V, *Bull 1454*: for this and extracts later in this chapter, Kidd, *Documents* III, pp. 220–222)

Here Pope Nicholas was referring to the long campaign to clear the Muslim invaders, often called Moors, from the whole Spanish peninsula, including Portugal (see p. 187). This task was nearing completion in his time. He continued:

> 'Also to those who conquer them, their kingdoms, and dwellings in far distant places, till now unknown.'

The Portuguese, having cleared their own country, had taken to the sea, and were pursuing the Moors southwards down the African coast. The Pope then took up the subject of:

> 'That noble man, Henry Prince of Portugal, uncle of our dearly beloved son in Christ, Alfonso King of Portugal.'

This was the prince whom history calls Henry the Navigator, in spite of the fact that he hardly ever went to sea. He distinguished himself in 1415, when the Portuguese captured Ceuta from the Moors, their first bit of African territory, opposite Gibraltar. Then in 1418 Prince Henry settled at Sagres, where Portugal's south-western tip juts into the Atlantic Ocean. There he spent the rest of his life, looking out to sea, watching ships, studying maps, and planning exploration further and further down Africa's coasts. He had to persuade and encourage

12.2 Prince Henry of Portugal, 'whom history calls Henry the Navigator', spent twenty-five years organizing voyages of discovery to Africa and towards the Indies, hoping to defeat the Moors and spread the Christian faith. This portrait is a detail from a painting by Nuño Goncalves.

his captains, and sometimes just shut his ears to their fears. For Portuguese sailors had heard of a 'giant hand of Satan raised above the waves' to seize any that sailed too far south, and Arabs described tropic seas where the water did really boil. Pope Nicholas mentioned none of this, but went on:

'Prince Henry never ceased for twenty-five years to send swift ships to search the sea and coasts . . . and so they came at last to Guinea . . . and later to the mouth of a great river supposed to be the Nile . . . taking possession of several islands . . . We hope the people may be converted and many souls won for Christ.'

'THE DISCOVERY OF GUINEA'

Fortunately we can still look at the book which the Pope had just read, with 'great joy'. It was written by Azurara in 1453 and was called, *The Discovery of Guinea*. The Pope was writing in 1454. 'Guinea' is a corruption of the name Ghana, then used for the area lying between the river Senegal and the river Niger. Azurara says that Prince Henry had five motives for organizing these voyages, (1) discovery, meaning not only discovery of Africa, but of a way round Africa to 'the Indies'; (2) commerce; (3) testing the strength of the enemy, i.e. the Moors; (4) the hope of finding a Christian ally; (5) desire to spread the Christian Faith.

The curious mention of the river 'supposed to be the Nile' refers to the river Senegal, where, after the long Sahara desert coastline, fertility begins again. Arab geographers had called it 'the Nile that flows west', and believed that it came from the same source as the Nile which flows north through Egypt, and one of whose sources, the Blue Nile, waters the Christian kingdom of Ethiopia.

The Portuguese of this period often repeated the hope about Prester John which had first been circulating three hundred years before (see p. 77). They interpreted it as meaning not east Asia but east Africa—a Christian kingdom beyond the Muslims, i.e. Ethiopia. The fourth of Prince Henry's five motives, according to Azurara's list, also refers to this hope.

The Portuguese did not yet know how far to the south the African continent extended, and were hoping, now that they had passed the Sahara Desert, that they might soon link up with fellow Christians on Africa's eastern side. Thus the Muslim barrier would be broken, and the Christian Faith could move freely eastward across the world.

Pope Nicholas concluded:

'The Prince (Henry) has rightly taken possession of the Moors' islands, lands, harbours, and seas . . . King Alfonso has the right to build churches and monasteries throughout provinces, islands, and places acquired, and yet to be acquired, and to send clergy who are willing to go, and who have the licence of their superiors.' (Nicholas V, *Bull 1454*, abbreviated)

The Pope had tried, the year before, to raise a Crusade, and had failed. Here he seemed to be realizing that the centuries-long struggle by Christians of Portugal against the Muslim invader had been a crusade, a crusade which was continuing as they now swept the seas clear of the same Muslim power.

One wishes he had lived a few years longer to see the development of this Christian recovery. For the Portuguese pushed on. In 1462 they reached Sierra Leone; in 1471 they crossed the equator. In 1482 an expedition founded the first European settlement on the Gold Coast, not only planting the flag of Portugal but celebrating the first Mass in West Africa, and praying for its people. By 1484 they had reached the Congo, and in 1487 Bartholomew Diaz rounded the Cape of Good Hope. Good hope indeed! Beyond lay a route which would pass around the Muslim barrier, and lead to the desired 'Indies'.

VASCO DA GAMA (1497)

The crowning achievement was in 1497–1498. Vasco da Gama after reaching the Cape of Good Hope sailed on to Mozambique, and then crossed the Arabian Sea to Calicut. It was the greatest feat in the whole history of seamanship up to this time. We saw in Volume 1 (p. 6 and map, p. 110) that according to *Periplous*, the book called *The Voyage* written in AD 60, there was Arab shipping off the east African coasts, and going across to India. The Portuguese now found the Arabs in control of trade routes right across Asia, with Calicut as the centre of their sea-power.

The Portuguese soon recognized that to remain in these waters they had to challenge Arab control, by taking Calicut and all its approaches. Within a few years the Portuguese had occupied Aden, Hormuz, and Malacca, key ports to the Red Sea, the Persian Gulf, and the China Sea, respectively.

These Portuguese blows to Arab-sea power were recognized as a crusade both by the Sultan of Egypt and in Rome. The Sultan at one stage threatened to seize the holy places in Jerusalem if the Portuguese did not cease their attacks. In Rome there was thanksgiving for the Christian capture of Malacca, and a procession in which the Pope himself took part.

Setback and recovery: the setback in the east had been a big one, and this recovery deserved a louder *Te Deum* than it received.

Labels within the illustration:
fulgur
S. Sophia
Johes bap̃
S. Johes Crisostoma
Domus mag̃ turci
Destructo antiqua
S. onofrius̃
Tabula mundo: u
Tabula equoni
Laonius turristanus filis̃
Laonius turristanus filis̃
Mariana
S. gromus

12.3 'By 1453 the army of the Turks was ready to finish its task: Constantinople fell. The church of the Holy Wisdom became a Muslim mosque.' (p. 172)
This picture from the Nuremburg Chronicles shows Constantinople under Turkish domination in 1493, with the palace of the Grand Turk to the right of St Sophia. The ship in the foreground is like those used by the Portuguese for their voyages.

12.4 The smaller picture shows a similar ship under sail.

COLUMBUS AND THE NEW WORLD (1492)

There was another attempt to find a way to the 'Indies' in spite of the Muslim barrier. This time the route was not southward round Africa, but westward round the world—and it was taken by men who were willing to gamble their lives on the world's being round. This was a short and simple voyage compared with some made by the Portuguese, but it is more famous in history, because of its surprising results.

Columbus, a Genoese sailor in the service of the King of Spain, reported in 1492:

'Thirty-three days after leaving Cadiz, I reached the Indian Sea, where I discovered many islands. To the first I gave the name San Salvador (Spanish, "Holy Saviour"), relying upon whose protection I had come hither.'

We smiled before (p. 182), at the Portuguese explorers' ignorance of geography, thinking at the river Senegal that they were not too far from Africa's southern tip, and so being wrong by more than half a continent. Columbus's mistake in calling this sea 'Indian'—and to the end of his life he thought the land he discovered was India—was the biggest mistake ever made in geography. He was wrong about the country, wrong about the continent, even wrong about the hemisphere. And in talking of 'West Indies' and 'American Indian' we have perpetuated the mistake. Columbus's landing was in the Caribbean, whose inhabitants, he said, were simple people, ready to exchange products of their own for a plate, a glass, a metal key, things which were new to them. His report continued:

'I myself gave them much and took nothing in return. I did this to pacify them, and that they might be led to become Christians. Let Christ rejoice in the salvation of the souls of so many nations hitherto lost. Let us all rejoice, both for the exultation of our Faith, and for the increase of our wealth.'

A new route to the Indies, and Columbus thought that he had found it! The truth was gradually recognized: what he had found was a new world!

In passing we should note another mistake: Columbus's too easy coupling of the 'exaltation of our Faith' with the 'increase of our wealth'. These two do not always easily go together.

One further voyage we must mention, though it did not take place until after the end of the fifteenth century—Magellan's voyage which crowned the discoveries of both Portugal and Spain. Magellan was a Portuguese, but he sailed under the flag of Spain. His ships in the years

1519–1522 passed through the straits at the American continent's southern tip which now bear his name, crossed the Pacific Ocean, reached the long-sought India, and became the first to sail round the globe.

As the new age, the modern age, *our* age opened, we may say that, whatever achievements the centuries ahead might see or not see, they would for the first time give to Christian people the chance literally to fulfil the Church's commission: 'Go ye into all the world.'

STUDY SUGGESTIONS

WORD STUDY

1. (a) What does the word 'renaissance' mean?
   (b) What two other names are often given to the event in European history called the 'Renaissance', i.e. when the literature, art, and thought of ancient Greece and Rome were rediscovered?

REVIEW OF CONTENT

2. Draw a time-line, divided into fifty-year sections, to cover the 1,000 years from AD 500 to AD 1500. Write in at the appropriate dates the chief events in the history of the Church during this period, as outlined on pp. 175–176.
3. What was the condition, by the year 1500 of:
   (a) The Syriac Church of the East?
   (b) The Greek Church?
   (c) The Church of the West?
4. 'Nicholas V was the best of the Renaissance Popes.' (p. 177) List some of his actions to illustrate this statement.
5. (a) Who was the scholar who proved that the *Donation of Constantine* was not a genuine document?
   (b) What difference, if any, did this make to the Papacy?
6. (a) Which nation was the first to use printing?
   (b) When was the art of printing first introduced to the West, and where in Europe was it first used?
   (c) What change did the introduction of printing bring about in people's everyday lives?
   (d) What change did it bring about in the life of the Church?
7. (a) For what purpose besides exploration were the Portuguese making voyages southwards down the African coast at the beginning of the fifteenth century?
   (b) Who was Henry the Navigator?
   (c) What five reasons for organizing voyages were attributed to Henry the Navigator by the author of the book *The Discovery of Guinea*?

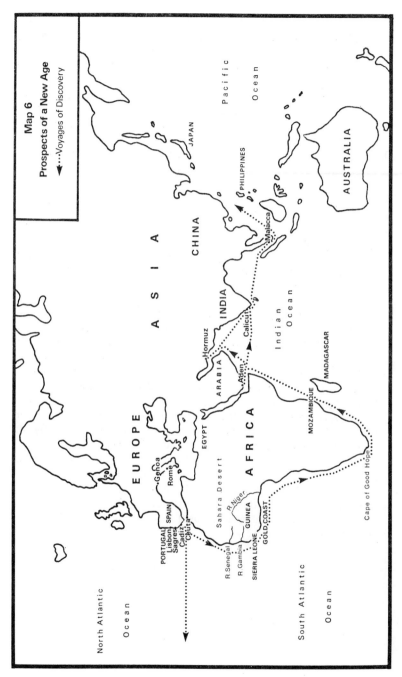

Map 6

Prospects of a New Age

•••Voyages of Discovery

8. (a) Who was the first navigator to round the Cape of Good Hope, and in what year?
   (b) Who was the first navigator to reach India by way of the Cape Good Hope, and in what year?
   (c) Why were these voyages to India by way of Africa so important?
   (d) What more had the Portuguese to do after reaching India?
9. What was the 'mistake' which Columbus made after crossing the Atlantic ocean, and in what ways has it been perpetuated?
10. Which navigator did in the end find a route to India by travelling westwards, and in what year?

DISCUSSION AND RESEARCH

11. 'The *Donation of Constantine*, which had been regarded as the authority for many powers claimed by the Pope, was nothing but make-believe.' (p. 177)
    From what 'authority' do bishops and other Church leaders in your country claim their powers today? Do you think that that authority is valid? If asked to do so, how could the Church prove its validity?
12. Can you think of any twentieth-century invention which could have as great an influence on the spread of Christian and other teaching as the introduction of printing to Europe did in the fifteenth century? Has it had such an influence? If not, why not?
13. 'The route westwards to "India" was taken by men who were willing to gamble on the world being round.' (p. 185)
    What 'gambles' of this kind, if any, have been made by explorers in more recent times? Have they been made 'for the exaltation of the Faith'—or for some other reason? What effect, if any, do you think they have had on the spread of Christianity?
14. 'The Pope hoped to bring the Church into harmony with the Renaissance, and perhaps encourage it to take the lead in this new learning' (p. 177). But some Christians have said that the Church should have had nothing to do with Renaissance learning, because it was based on the pagan ideas of ancient Greece and Rome.
    What is your opinion?

Key to Study Suggestions

(NB Line numbering refers to *text*, including quotations but excluding headings)
CHAPTER 1

1. See p. 1 line 4.
2. (a) See p. 4 para. 1.
   (b) See p. 4 para. 4.
3. See p. 7 last para. and p. 8 first 3 lines.
4. See p. 7 para. 3 lines 2 and 3, and para. 4 line 4.
5. (a) See p. 1 para. 1 line 6.
   (b) See p. 1 lines 12–18.
   (c) See p. 1 lines 23–29.
6. See p. 2 para. 5.
7. See p. 2 para. 6.
8. See p. 4 paras 2 and 3.
9. See p. 4 paras 2, 3, and 4.
10. (a) See p. 5 paras 1 and 2.
    (b) See p. 5 lines 2 and 3.
11. See p. 5 last para. and p. 6 para. 1.
12. See p. 7 lines 15–25.
13. (a) See p. 5 para. 4.
15. (a) See p. 8 para. 2, quotation.
16. Based on pp. 4, 5, and 6.
17. See p. 5 para. 4.

CHAPTER 2

1. See p. 12 para. 5.
2. (a) See p. 14 line 15.
   (b) See p. 16 lines 11–13.
   (c) See p. 16 para. numbered 2, last 6 lines.
3. (a) See p. 11 paras 1–3.
   (b) See p. 11 para. 4 lines 1–4.
4. See p. 12 paras 2 and 3.
5. (a) See p. 12 paras 3 and 6.
   (b) See p. 12 paras 4 and 5.
6. (a) See p. 13 paras 2 and 5.
   (b) and (c) See p. 13 para. 2.
7. (a) See p. 13 para. 3.
   (b) See p. 13 para. 4.
8. See p. 14 paras 1 and 2.

9. See p. 14 last 11 lines.

10. Base your work on p. 14, section headed 'The Arab Invasions'.

11. (a) See p. 19 lines 2–5.

(b) There are many differences. One obvious one is that the *Koran* consists of Muhammad's teachings, written down in his lifetime, while the Bible contains many other books, e.g. of history and prophecy, written at different times, besides the teachings of Jesus.

12. Some points of outward likeness are:

Jesus and Muhammad both called their followers to worship and obey God. They both withdrew into the wilderness (desert) for a time.

They both treated poor people and slaves as equals.

They both preached against wealth and extravagance.

Some points of unlikeness are:

Muhammad was not only a religious leader, he accepted political leadership and authority; Jesus never sought power for Himself.

Muhammad had a wealthy wife, and several children; Jesus 'had not where to lay His head'.

Muhammad led his followers in battle; Jesus preached peace.

Muhammad died successful and honoured; Jesus was put to death as a criminal.

13. See pp. 18 and 19.

CHAPTER 3

1. See p. 24 para. 2.

2. (a) See p. 22 para. 3 and p. 26 paras 3 and 4.

(b) See p. 30 lines 21–23.

(c) See p. 24 para. 1.

(d) See p. 24 line 18.

(e) See p. 30 lines 23 and 24.

3. (a)–(e) See p. 22 lines 16–29.

4. (a) and (b) See p. 23 section headed 'Patrick, Apostle of Ireland',

5. See p. 24 lines 25 and 26.

6. See p. 24 last para.

7. See p. 26 section headed 'The Roman Mission'.

8. See p. 7 lines 30–32, p. 8 lines 3–8, and p. 27 lines 1–9.

9. You could check your own work by reference to the whole section headed 'Augustine, First Archbishop of Canterbury', pp. 26–29.

10. (a) See p. 29 para. 3.

(b) See p. 2 para. 5 and p. 29 para. 2.

11. See p. 29 last 10 lines and p. 31 lines 6–12.

12. (a) See p. 31 lines 24–34.

(b) See p. 33, all four quotations from Bede's *Ecclesiastical History*.

13. See p. 24 lines 1–3, p. 31 last 4 lines, and p. 32 lines 1 and 2.

14. (a) See p. 33 last 2 lines and p. 34 lines 1–6.

(b) See p. 34 lines 6–31.

15. (a) See p. 22 lines 8 and 9 from foot, and p. 34 section heading.

(b) See p. 35 lines 14–17.

(c) See p. 35 line 18.

16. See p. 35 lines 20–28.
17. (a) You could check your work by reference to p. 35 last 6 lines and p. 36 lines 1–3.
    (b) See p. 36 para. 2.
18. (a) See p. 36 para. 3.
    (b) See p. 36 section heading.
19. See p. 36 last 13 lines.
22. Based on p. 2 para. 5 and p. 29 para. 2.

CHAPTER 4

1. (a) See p. 40.
   (b) See p. 40 para. 4.
2. (a) Scholar, wise man.
   (b) royal family, ruling family.
3. See p. 43 last para.
4. (a) and (b) See p. 40 para. 1.
   (c) and (d) See p. 40 para. 2.
5. See p. 40 last line and p. 41 lines 1–19.
6. See p. 41 lines 6–19.
7. (a) and (b) See p. 42 lines 16–27 and Vol. 1, p. 141.
8. (a), (b), (c) See p. 43, section headed '(d) The Work of Christ'.
9. See p. 40 para. 2 and p. 44 last 5 lines.
10. (a) and (b) See p. 45 para. 2.
11. (a) See p. 41 lines 21–23.
    (b) See p. 45 last para. and p. 46.
12. You could check your work by reference to p. 48 paras 1 and 2.
13. See p. 48 paras 2 and 3.
14. (a) See p. 48 para. 3.
    (b) See p. 48 last line and p. 49 lines 1–27.
    (c) See p. 49 lines 19–27.
15. (a) See p. 49 last 12 lines and p. 50 lines 1–20.
    (b) See p. 50 lines 21–28.
16. See p. 51 paras 2, 3, and 4.

CHAPTER 5

1. (a) See p. 63 lines 11–3 from foot.
   (b) See p. 64 lines 3–5.
   (c) See p. 63 lines 7–3 from foot, p. 66 lines 13–28, p. 68 lines 9–27, and map 4 p. 69.
2. *Preacher*: preceptor, prelate, presbyter, predicator, pastor
   Predator: pirate, pillager, peculator, raptor
3. (a) See p. 60 lines 5–7.
   (b) See p. 60 lines 7–10.
4. See p. 56 para. 1.
5. See p. 56 line 17—p. 57 line 2.

6. (a) See p. 57 lines 8–21.
   (b) See p. 57 lines 22–34.
7. See p. 58 lines 26–30.
8. (a) and (b) See p. 58 last 3 paras.
9. (a) and (b) See p. 57 last para. to p. 59 line 5 from foot.
10. See p. 60 para. 3 last line.
11. See p. 60 paras 3 and 4.
12. See p. 61 lines 20–24.
13. See p. 60 last para, and p. 63 lines 1–19.
14. See p. 61 numbered paras 1 and 2.
15. See p. 63 last 2 paras and p. 64 lines 1–5.
16. (a) See p. 63 lines 5–10
    (b) See p. 64 para. 3 and last para. and p. 65 para. 1.
    (c) See p. 65 para. 2.
    (d) See p. 66 lines 11–3 from foot.
    (e) See p. 67 para. 2 to p. 68 line 5.
17. (a) and (b) See p. 67 para. 4.
18. (a) See p. 66 lines 11–6 from foot.
    (b) See p. 67 para. 3.
19. (a) See p. 68 last 3 paras.
    (b) See p. 68 last 3 lines and p. 70.
    (c) See p. 68 last para.
23. Based on p. 70 quotations.

CHAPTER 6

1. (a) See p. 74 lines 6 and 7.
   (b) You could check your work by reference to p. 74 paras 2 and 3.
2. See p. 73 para. 2 lines 3–6.
3. (a) and (b) See p. 73 para. 1.
4. (a) and (b) See p. 73 para. 2.
5. See p. 73 last line and p. 74 lines 1–3.
6. (a) See p. 74 para. 5.
   (b) See p. 77 last 2 paras.
   (c) See p. 77 paras 3 and 4.
   (d) See p. 77 last para.
7. See p. 74 para. 4.
8. (a) and (b) See p. 74 para. 5.
9. See p. 74 last 4 lines and p. 76 lines 1–8.
10. (a) and (b) See p. 76 para. 3.
11. (a) See p. 76 para. 4.
    (b) See p. 76 last para. and p. 77 lines 1–4.
12. (a) See p. 77 last 3 lines and p. 79 lines 1–7.
    (b) See p. 80 para. 1.
13. (a) and (b) See p. 80 para. 2.

14. See p. 8 lines 15–8 from foot.

15. You could check your work by reference to p. 80 last para., p. 81 lines 1–6, and the section headed 'The Roman Mission', pp. 24–29.

16. See p. 83 paras 2 and 3.

17. (a) See p. 84 paras 2–5.
    (b) See p. 84 para. 6.
    (c) See p. 85 paras 1 and 2.

18. See p. 85 lines 15–26.

19. See p. 85 para. 1.

20. (a) and (b) See p. 85 last 2 paras.
    (c) See p. 86.

21. (a) See p. 86 lines 12–8 from foot.
    (b) See p. 86 last 7 lines and p. 87 paras 1 and 2.

22. (a) See p. 84 para. 4 and p. 87 last para.
    (b) See p. 85 lines 9 and 10, and p. 89 lines 3–7.
    (c) See p. 89 section headed '2. Learning'.
    (d) See p. 90 section headed '3. Life', especially last 2 lines.

23. (a) See p. 89 para. 3.

24. (a) You could check your work by reference to p. 81 and p. 83 paras 1 and 2.

25. (a) See p. 83 para. 3.

27. (a) See p. 86 lines 21 and 22.

CHAPTER 7

1. (a) See p. 96 lines 10 and 11.
   (b) See p. 97 last para.
   (c) and (d) See p. 99 lines 3–8.
   (e) See p. 101 last para.

2. (a) and (d) See p. 1–6 para. 5.
   (b) See p. 106 last para. and p. 107 first para.
   (e) See p. 108 last line and p. 109 lines 1 and 2.

3. See p. 94 last para. and p. 96 lines 1–3.

4. See p. 96 para. 2.

5. (a) See p. 96 last 3 paras p. 97, and p. 98 para. 1.

6. (a) See p. 98 last para. and p. 99 paras 1–4.
   (b) See p. 98 last para. but one.

7. See p. 99 lines 17–12 from foot.

8. (a) See p. 1–3 last 3 paras and p. 104 lines 1–6.
   (b) See p. 104 lines 6–9.
   (c) See p. 104 paras 2 and 3.

9. See p. 104 last para.

10. (a) See p. 105 numbered paras 1–3 at foot of page.
    (b) See p. 106 para. 2.
    (c) See p. 106 para. 4.

11. See p. 106 first and last paras, p. 108 and p. 109.

12. See p. 106 last para., p. 108 first and last paras, and p. 109.

13. (a) See p. 98 para. 1.

15. (a) See p. 109 lines 10–15.

CHAPTER 8

1. See p. 119 para. 3.

2. (a) and (b) See p. 119 paras 3–6.

3. (a) See p. 112 paras 1–3.
   (b) See p. 112 para. 1. and p. 116 para. 5.

4. See p. 119 paras 4 and 7 and p. 122 paras 2 and 3.

5. (a) See section headings pp. 112, 114, 115, and 116.
   (b) See especially p. 112 paras 1–3 (to answer the question fully you need to work carefully through pp. 112–119 line 5).

6. (a) See p. 112 last line, p. 113 lines 1–12, and last para., and p. 114 lines 1–13.
   (b) See p. 113 para. 4.
   (c) See p. 113 para. 5—p. 114 line 13.

7. (a) See p. 114 para. 3.
   (b) See p. 114 para. 4.
   (c) See p. 114 last 8 lines and p. 115 lines 1–4.

8. (a) See p. 115 line 13.
   (b) See p. 115, whole section on Peter Lombard.

9. (a) See p. 115 line 5 from foot.
   (b) See p. 116 last 2 lines.

10. See p. 115 last 7 lines and p. 116 paras 1–3.

11. (a) See p. 116 last 2 paras.
    (b) Compare, e.g. p. 84 lines 14–18 and 26 and 27 with p. 116 lines 29–31 and 11–7 from foot.
    (c) Compare, e.g. p. 89 lines 11–9 from foot with p. 117 lines 3–5 and 21–24.
    (d) See p. 117 lines 3–12 and 21–23.
    (e) See p. 117 last para. but one.

12. (a) See p. 119 paras 5 and 6.
    (b) See p. 120 para. 4.
    (c) See p. 120 para. 5 and p. 121 paras 2 and 3.

13. See p. 120 para. 2.

14. Compare p. 119 paras 4–6 with p. 121 last para. and p. 122 para. 1.

15. (a) See p. 114 para. 4.
    (b) See p. 114 para. 5.

16. (a) See p. 120 para. 3.

17. See p. 98 last para. and p. 99.

18. See p. 121 para. 3.

CHAPTER 9

1. See p. 130 lines 8–2 from foot.

2. See p. 128 para. 2.

3. (a) and (b) See p. 128 para. 2—p. 129 line 2.

4. See p. 129 para. 4.

5. See p. 129 paras 3 and 5 and p. 130 para. 1.

6. (a) See p. 130 para. 2.
   (b) See p. 130 para. 3.

7. (a) See p. 130 para. 3—p. 131 line 2.
   (b) See p. 131 lines 3 and 4.

8. (a) See p. 131 paras 3–6 and p. 132 lines 1 and 2 and para. 5.
   (b) See p. 131 para. 5.

9. (a) See p. 132 para. 2.
   (b) See p. 132 para. 3.

10. (a) and (b) See p. 132 last para. and p. 63 para. 1.
    (c) See p. 132 last line and p. 133 lines 1–4.

11. You could check your work by reference to p. 133 para. 2—p. 134 last line but one.

12. See p. 136 paras 2 and 3, and p. 112 last para. to p. 114 line 4.

13. (a) See p. 136 last 3 lines and p. 137 lines 1–8.
    (b) See p. 137 paras 2 and 3.

14. (a) and (b) See p. 137 para. 4.

15. (a) See p. 137 last 2 paras and p. 138 para. 1.
    (b) See p. 137 para. 5.

16. (a) and (b) See p. 139 para. 4 and p. 140 paras 1 and 2.

CHAPTER 10

1. (a) See p. 143 last line but one.
   (b) See p. 147 para. 2.
   (c) See p. 149 para. 2.
   (d) See p. 144 para. 1.

2. (a) See p. 143 para. 3.
   (b) See p. 143 para. 4.

3. (a) See p. 143 last para.
   (b) See p. 144 last para.
   (c) See p. 144 last line and p. 145 lines 1–15.
   (d) See p. 145 last line and p. 147 lines 1–5.
   (e) See p. 144 para. 1. and Chart 3.

4. See p. 147 para. 3.

5. See p. 147 para. 4.

6. (a) See p. 148 para. 2.
   (b) See p. 148 para. 3.

7. (a) See p. 143 last para.
   (b) See p. 148 last para. line 6.
   (c) See p. 148 last para. lines 6–8.

8. (a) See p. 149 line 8.
   (b) See p. 149 lines 8–14.

9. See p. 149 last para. but one.

10. (a), (b), (c), and (d) See p. 150 para. 2.

11. See p. 150 paras 4, 5, and 6.

12. (a) See p. 85 para. 3 and p. 150 para. 4.
(b) You could check your work by reference to the long quotation from *The Little Flowers* on p. 151.

13. (a) and (b) See p. 153 para. 2 and 3.
(c) See p. 154 lines 2–4.
(d) See p. 154 lines 6–8.

14. (a) and (b) See p. 154 para. 4.
(c) See p. 155 para. 2.

15. (a) See p. 155 section heading.
(b) See p. 155 para. 3 last 2 lines.
(c) See p. 155 last 2 lines and p. 156 paras 1–4.
(d) See p. 156 para. 4 lines 4–7.

16. (a) See p. 157 last para. and p. 158 para. 1.
(b) See p. 158 para. 3.

20. Based on p. 144 Chart 3.

21. See p. 155 paras 4 and 5.

CHAPTER 11

1. See p. 165 para. 4 lines 8–13.

2. See p. 165 para. 1.

3. (a) and (b) See p. 161 Chart 4.

4. (a) See p. 162 para. 3.
(b) See p. 162 last 3 paras.

5. (a) See p. 162 paras 4 and 5.
(b) See p. 164 para. 2.

6. (a) See p. 162 para. 5.
(b) See p. 164 para. 1.

7. (a) See p. 164 para. 3.
(b) See p. 164 para. 4.
(c) See p. 164 para. 5.

8. See p. 164 last 2 paras.

9. See p. 165 paras 2 and 3.

10. See p. 165 para. 3 last 3 lines.

11. See section headings pp. 166 and 168, p. 165 last para., p. 166 paras. 1 and 3, and p. 168 para. 4.

12. (a) See p. 166 para. 2.
(b) See p. 166 para. 3.

13. See p. 167 para. 2.

14. (a) and (b) See p. 167 para. 4.
(c) and (d) See p. 167 last para. and p. 168 paras 1 and 2.

15. See p. 168 para. 5.

16. See p. 170 paras. 5 and 6.

17. See p. 171 para. 3.

18. (a) See p. 171 last para.

(b) See p. 171 last para. and p. 172 para. 1.
(c) See p. 172 para. 2.

19. (a) and (b) See p. 172 para. 3.
(c) See p. 172 para. 4. last 2 lines.

22. (a) See p. 170 section headed 'Rodrigo Borgia'.

CHAPTER 12

1. (a) See p. 176 para. 7.
(b) See p. 176 section heading.

3. (a) See p. 176 numbered para. 1.
(b) See p. 176 numbered para. 2.
(c) See p. 176 numbered para. 3.

4. See p. 177 para. 1.

5. (a) and (b) See p. 177 para. 2.

6. (a) and (b) See p. 177 last para.
(c) See p. 179 para. 1.

7. (a) See p. 180 para. 4.
(b) See p. 182 last para. but one.
(c) See p. 182 para. 2.

8. (a) See p. 183 para. 2.
(b) See p. 183 para. 3.
(c) See p. 183 para. 3 last 3 lines.
(d) See p. 183 paras 4 and 5.

9. See p. 185 para. 3.

10. See p. 185 last para. and p. 186 para. 1.

Index

INDEX